Jules Henry
on Education

Also by Jules Henry

Pathways to Madness
Culture Against Man
Jungle People: A Kaingáng Tribe of the Highlands of Brazil

Jules Henry
on Education

Random House New York

Contents

44034

Jules Henry
on Education

| Vulnerability in Education*

This paper would never have been written were it not for Raymond Callahan's distinguished book *Education and the Cult of Efficiency*,† in which he discusses the extreme vulnerability of school administrators. He argues that, up to the second decade of this century, they were vulnerable largely because of the power exercised over education by business. Reading the book, I said to myself: 'All are vulnerable. Mankind is a vulnerable animal and suffers from feelings of vulnerability day in, day out, awake and in his dreams.'

As a college teacher, I am aware of the excruciating vulnerability of students; and my own sensation of vulnerability as a student will never leave me. I am remotely like the old professor in the movie *Wild Strawberries* who, at the peak of his fame, when he was about to receive the highest scholastic honour in the country and a salute of cannons, had a dream the night before of failing an examination. It is not very long since I ceased to have such dreams; they are the primeval dreams of confronting life's test and failing.

Social scientists consider protection a requisite for society, but it is also essential that society make men vulnerable. If a man is invulnerable society cannot reach him, and if society produces men who cannot be reached it cannot endure. Thus society will protect us only if we consent to being relatively defenceless. To the end that man can be injured and thus brought to heel, an array of frightful devices has been created so that men will be meek and mild, even to being meek and mild in order to be violent and terrible, like the soldier who obeys orders to kill. From all this it follows that in order for society to survive it must create a vulnerable character structure in its members. The

*From *Teachers College Record*, vol. 68, no. 2, November 1966.
†Raymond Callahan, *Education and the Cult of Efficiency*, University of Chicago Press, 1964.

combination of factors that make us thus vulnerable I call the *vulnerability system*.

Bringing men to heel

Where is man vulnerable and how is his vulnerability accomplished? To begin with we must have a clear idea of the areas of existence in which man is exposed to injury. First there is his reputation – his good name. Since a person protects it by learning the norms of his social class and never deviating, reputation depends on careful study of norms and obedience to them, however one may despise them. Of course it is always better if one believes in them, and this is the effortless way of maintaining a good reputation; of being socially invulnerable. But maintaining a good reputation must involve also a certain amount of concealment – of hiding one's deviations. Since deviation can be in thought as well as in action, invulnerability of reputation involves learning how to conceal deviant thoughts. Hence the person with an invulnerable reputation knows how to conceal his socially unacceptable thoughts – if he ever has any. Of course, the best way to handle deviant thoughts is NOT to have any. This requires either looking away quickly from the socially unpleasant; or better still, never looking at anything closely.

How does society make people excruciatingly sensitive to the possibilities of and dangers in losing reputation, and how does society make one sensitive to one's vulnerability? It is done through placing reputation – the social person – in the centre of consideration and making reputation destiny; by degrading the inner self to second, third, or merely adventitious place, and making the social façade supreme, so that at every step the self will be sacrificed to the façade.

How is this manoeuvre accomplished? Surely it can be accomplished best through acquiescence and through disregarding and even punishing the emerging self. It is not so much, however, that the child is punished for asserting his selfhood, but that the thrusting upward of the self is not even seen; what is seen by the parent is largely what is relevant to social requirements; what contributes to a good name; what makes one socially invulnerable. In this way the spirit is pruned, largely insensibly, of everything that is not socially acceptable and self becomes identical with reputation. This need not be so, for it is possible for a person to lose his good name and yet accomplish good things in the name of his self. Great reformers and creators have often done this.

Dependence and inflated images

An important function of the feeling of vulnerability is to make us dependent. As small children we are overwhelmed by our vulnerability and so lean on parents, who have in this way become exalted in our eyes. Thus another function of vulnerability is to enlarge the image of those who could harm us and those who protect us. Society is built on a foundation of inflated images derived from vulnerability and upheld by the feeling that what is important are the norms and not ourselves.

While in our culture dependence on parents is necessary and very real in childhood, the function of the inflated parental image is to project the child's feeling of vulnerability far beyond the boundaries of realism – in order that society itself may be protected. Thus behind every inflated authority image lies society's fear that it is vulnerable. Behind every inflated image lies society's determination to cancel independence. The child's vulnerability is sustained and intensified by the elementary school, where he is at the teacher's mercy. The teacher, clearly through no fault of her own, is the agent of vulnerability; and she transmits the sense of vulnerability to the child through two weapons thrust into her hands, sometimes against her will – discipline and the power to fail the child. Before these absolute weapons the child is even more vulnerable than with his parents; for with his parents the agony of vulnerability is allayed in part by love, and he can, within limits, fight back. In school, however, this usually is not the case; for in the first place, in the contemporary overcrowded class room, fighting back is a negation of necessary order and routine, and fear of failure is the pulse of school life. Remove the fear of failure and education in America would stop as if its heart had been cut out. Yet we cannot blame the feeling of vulnerability on fear of failure, for after all, without fear of failure nobody would try for success, and without striving for success there could be no contemporary culture. Thus another characteristic of vulnerability – its roots in the idea of success.

The lifetime fears

Fear of failure does not begin in school, for in our culture even the basic biological functions of early childhood are amalgamated with the ideas of success and failure. Moving one's bowels at the right time and in the right place is a great success for a baby; while losing control and doing it on the living-room rug is a failure, a source of shame and disgrace for many children. Even taking the right amount of milk from the bottle, and eating all one's spinach before getting dessert are successes, while leaving food on one's plate, or eating sloppily so that milk dribbles on one's shirt may be considered failures. Thus a baby is already psychologicaly vulnerable at the mouth and bowel, and thus in our culture fear of failure is built right into the biological functions. In this way the soul is prepared for the intensified fear of failure instilled all through school, including college and graduate school.

Related to such fears is the college student's query of 'Will I make it?', and for many college is a four-year opium sleep in which the answer to the question is postponed, while the student commits himself to the pleasures of a coeducational school as a courting pavilion, while at the same time trying to make himself invulnerable to the dangers of the socio-economic system. And this is the paradox – that even as the undergraduate is presumably arming, he gives himself up to pleasure in order to forget the enemy.

Thus fear of failure is the dark aspect of the hope and striving for success. For most of us, our abilities, our good looks and our social techniques – our pleasant, public relations 'hellos', our ability to laugh at anybody's jokes, our capacity to hold conventional opinions and never to value or fight for any position in an argument too much – never seem quite adequate to ward off all the chances of failure. If a young person is successful in competition for one grade, one scholarship, one boy or girl, or one position today, can he be sure of being successful next time? In our culture a person's armour of personal capabilities is never predictably adequate, so that like the stock market and the gross national product, one can never be sure that if his capabilities are high today they will not crash tomorrow.

From this long training in feeling vulnerable the graduate student enters the academic world with a greater concern with reputation than with self, and an overpowering fear of failure. Under these conditions he is bound to be a failure to his self and at this point the *coup de grâce* is often administered to it.

Vulnerability in the schools

In the world outside the university many institutions ensure that the sense of vulnerability will never be lost. Every teacher in a public school system, for example, knows that if he asserts his self the probabilities of getting a rise or even keeping his job are reduced. But behind the principal who makes this clear to him is a superintendent who can punish the principal; and behind the superintendent is a board of education, while behind them is a state department of education ready to punish them all. Behind the state department are the people. Now the circle is complete, for the people, after all, are interested largely in preserving their good names. Since so many among them have given up self-striving, why should they allow it to anybody else? Furthermore they are frightened about what might happen to their non-conforming children.

It is now time to ask: 'How shall a person who wishes to assert himself in the school system become invulnerable or at least reduce his vulnerability?' By self-assertion I do not necessarily mean yelling at the principal, although it is rarely that assertion of one's self does not entail standing up to a superior.

By assertion of the self, I mean doing and saying what is in harmony with a self that is striving for something significant, for something which would be a step in the direction of self-realization in the direction of something that would enable one to say to one's self, 'I have made myself more significant in my own eyes.' It is this 'ownmost self', as Martin Heidegger has called it, that studies and evaluates remorselessly, that I am talking about.

For a teacher, assertion of the self would involve saying what he thinks most enlightening to the students; refusing to use stupid books, or reinterpreting them to make sense; deviating from the embalmed curriculum, and so on. Alone, he obviously can do this only within limits – although, when we come to think of it, the country is so starved for teachers now that after a squabble a teacher can often go around the corner to the next school district and get another job; while principals who once never thought twice before letting a teacher go, now think a hundred times.

On the other hand, going it alone is foolish, not so much because of the teacher's vulnerability but because, if his ideas are good, other teachers should share and express them; and if the majority of teachers in the same school do, it is difficult to withstand them. If a teacher acts alone and is forced to lie down or quit, the sense of vulnerability is intensified throughout the school system. The sense of vulnerability functions in a school system to frighten the teachers into becoming stupid; and since when they become stupid, so do the pupils, we end up with the understanding that vulnerability in the teacher helps educate children to stupidity. In this way society gets what it wants.

The example of Paradise

The functioning of the vulnerability system is illustrated by the case of Virginia Franklin, a high-school teacher in Paradise, California, as reported in *Life*, 26 April 1963.
I quote from the article :

The rage in Paradise centres on a high-school teacher named Virginia Franklin. She believes America is served best by training children to make up their own minds. Her social-studies classes, filled with debate, are encouraged to read material of widely divergent points of view, from the liberal to the extremes of the right wing.

Although Mrs Franklin earned an award from the Freedoms Foundation, she gained the enmity of the local American Legion post and others, including the John Birch Society. She was, of course, accused of being a communist, and one of her students was discovered spying on her in class by means of a tape recorder hidden in a hole carved in a text book. Fortunately Mrs Franklin is such a good teacher that she had the support of her principal, her superintendent and a small majority of the people who voted in the election for a new member of the school board. Mrs Franklin's supporter won.

This case has many features of the vulnerability system as it operates in our country. It is seen to have its roots in irrational fear and hate, and it takes possession of a revered symbol, in this case love of country. But it appropriates the fear symbol also which, in this case, is communism, for the extreme right considers itself the sole defender of the country. Mrs Franklin would have been vulnerable had she stood alone; but what is most striking is that, although the principal, the superintendent and the school board supported her during the outbreak of lunacy, the other teachers did not come forward.

The comment of Dr George Baron of the Institute of Education of the University of London is vital in connection with the case. Writing in the *Teachers College Record* (May 1964), he says:

The Hell in Paradise case ... gives to an English reader at first the impression of a closed, insular little society in which all is distrust and suspicion ...

There was, it would seem, no structure of accepted authority and custom to which the participants could appeal, no firmly held views on what was the nature of the trust that parent, teacher and pupil must have in each other and in each other's roles, in the school situation. Moreover ... neither teacher nor principal was effectively supported by any professional associations; *no university appears to have lent its weight to the cause of the teacher's freedom, and no figures of significance in the intellectual and political life of the nation seized on the incident as one to be lifted out of its purely parochial context*. It was left then, for the ... small community of Paradise to decide unaided issues that have occupied men for centuries.

Thus Dr Baron sees to the core: the distrust and suspicion which spread like cancer; the readiness of hate and fear-motivated organizations to usurp power where no clear authority exists; and the oceanic lack of involvement of the American people in their own vulnerable predicament. This is brought out by Dr Baron's remarks that no professional association, no university – especially professors of education – came forward to be heard on the matter. Like the New Yorkers who watched from behind their blinds while a woman was stabbed to death, they remained uninvolved. As long as Americans are uninvolved in one another, each stands alone in his vulnerability. We conclude from this that a consequence of extreme vulnerability, wherein all men stand alone, is to make all men vulnerable; to bring all men to heel. Commenting further Dr Baron says:

This is markedly different from the situation in England – or, indeed, in Europe generally – where the universities, the schools, and the professions together have a coherence that protects them and individual teachers and practitioners from local and other external pressures.

In conclusion he says:

Given the place accorded to the local community in school affairs [in the United States], the isolation of the teacher, the seriousness of the heed paid to the views of children and adolescents, the political function ascribed to the school [as a controller of political ideas], and the fear of uncontrolled unusual ideas, other Paradises are inevitable. Teachers and parents who support mildly controversial ideas, even though they are commonplaces throughout the western world, must then live with the fear of being denounced and persecuted.

It is now necessary to ask the question, 'Where were the professors of education?' As a matter of fact, where are professors altogether in the social studies issue? We can examine some of the factors that might prevent them from taking strong positions on sharpening the social studies. In the first place the professors of education in those institutions which are in the most strategic position to make their opinions felt, are subject to the same pressures toward ineffectualness as Mrs Franklin. Their situation is aggravated, however, by the fact that although their universities may be tolerant, the state departments, fearful of their own position, cannot afford to liberalize the social studies, and therefore the professors cannot afford to be different.

The roots of incompetence

Since a consequence of vulnerability is to prevent social change, and since in our culture there is always a strong push for enlightened social change, we conclude that usually the function of the vulnerability system is to prevent enlightenment and the consequent change. Put another way, the function of the vulnerability system is often to guarantee darkness and incompetence. As a matter of fact, the people who are in the positions most strategic for social change are usually the most vulnerable. In government an outstanding example of this is the United States Department of Labour, which, although originally established to look after the interests of labour, was quickly deprived of power because of the danger of too great closeness of labour and government. Shorn of real power, the Department of Labor became a frozen bureaucracy dedicated largely to collecting statistics and keeping out of trouble with Congress, the Department of State and organized labour itself, who came to look upon the Department as largely a do-nothing outfit, uninterested in labour's welfare and under the thumb of Congress and business.

In education the group most strategic for social change is the teachers, and we know that the teachers are a vulnerable group. Fifty years ago labour was in a similar position, and it is only through organizing that it lost its vulnerability. As soon as this happened, however, labour lost interest in social change also. This suggests that although a vulnerable group cannot institute social change, once it has become invulnerable it may lose its interest in social change.

As a group becomes invulnerable, either through organization or through freezing in self-protective attitudes, it also becomes incompetent, because within the cake of protection that freezes around it there are frozen also the skills the group is seeking to protect. Hence teachers don't change, superintendents don't change, and workers do not take the trouble to educate themselves beyond the skills guaranteed to them by their organization. Over the years invulnerability through hiding has become the very factor that has now made educators increasingly vulnerable to the criticism of incompetence.

Scapegoats and children

In all of this those who suffer most are children, for the defensiveness of everybody — the socially patterned exposure and vulnerability of everybody in the educational system produces classrooms where off-beat questions are rarely asked. If they arise, they are ignored by the teacher; the readers, written largely by females who make a business of writing mindless stories, confront no issue but the apathy of the children; and, for generations, little changes but the faces.

Attacks on teachers nowadays therefore have some of the

spuriousness of attacks on Jews, for whenever a society is under stress the most vulnerable group becomes the scapegoat. Anti-educationalism is a refined form of scapegoating. In the present crisis in education, we see that what really binds the system is the hysterical and stingy public, committed to the high-rising living standard and frightened out of its wits by fear of communism. Meanwhile, in the drive to improve the teaching of science and mathematics we observe a present paradox, for while fear impels us to revolutionize science teaching the danger arises – as witness Mrs Franklin – that we go backwards in other areas. Even the fear of communism, however, is not the force behind the effort to improve the teaching of science and mathematics. Basically the force is all of business – textiles, oil, supermarkets, rockets and so on, who need the scientist and the mathematician to automate, to analyse, to invent and to compute along with the computers; for business is so vulnerable to competition, to obsolescence, to the stock market, to imports, to a labour movement and to depression that it needs our children's brains as protection. We must not, however, let everything else in our schools remain dead and embalmed while science and mathematics spring to a new and ambiguous life.

The case of René Descartes

Most of us have learned in introductory courses in philosophy that Descartes was so afraid of the church that he had to prove many times that God exists, that he withdrew several of his works on hearing of the condemnation of Galileo, and that he insisted on anonymity. It has not been pointed out that Descartes seems to have avoided discovering calculus because he was afraid that analysis of infinity would be considered blasphemy. Anyone who knows Descartes's capacities, that he started western philosophy on new pathways, that he is a fundamental source of modern phenomenology, and that he invented analytical geometry, could not doubt, after reading his *Principles*, that he could have discovered calculus had he not been afraid of inquiring into the nature of infinity. Consider the following from Principles XXVI and XXVII :

That we must not try to dispute about the infinite, but just consider that all that in which we find no limits is indefinite, such as the extension of the world, the divisibility of its parts, the number of the stars, etc.

We will thus never hamper ourselves with disputes about the infinite, since it would be absurd that we who are finite should undertake to decide anything regarding it. . . . That is why we do not care to reply to those who demand whether the half of an infinite line is infinite, and whether an infinite number is even or odd and so on. . . . And for our part, while we regard things in which, in a certain sense, we observe no limits, we shall not for all that state that they are infinite, but merely hold them to be indefinite. Thus because we cannot imagine an extension so great that we cannot at the same time conceive that there may be one yet greater, we shall say that the magnitude of possible things is indefinite.

Now come the lines that make clear that the calculus was definitely within Descartes's reach:

And because we cannot divide a body into parts which are so small that each part cannot be divided into others yet smaller, we shall consider that the quantity may be divided into parts whose number is indefinite.

Since infinity and the infinitesimal are at the core of the calculus and since Descartes discovered analytical geometry, necessary preliminary to calculus, it is highly probable he would have discovered calculus too if he had not been afraid. Principle XXVII makes the issue even clearer.

And we shall name these things indefinite rather than infinite in order to reserve to God alone the name of infinite, first of all because in Him alone we observe no limitation whatever, and because we are quite certain that He can have none. [I change now to the French translation, because the issues are clearer there.] * As regards other things we know that they are not thus absolutely perfect because although we observe in them certain properties which appear to have no limit, we yet know that this proceeds from our lack of understanding and not from their natures.

So, he says, man must leave the infinite and the infinitesimal unplumbed because they belong to God and are beyond under-

* See *Philosophical Works of Descartes*, translated into English by Elizabeth S. Haldane and G. R. T. Ross, Cambridge University Press, 1931. The translators indicate that Descartes was enthusiastic about the French translation (from Latin) and that he wrote the Preface.

standing – even though it was perfectly clear that Descartes understood them. Thus the sensation of vulnerability prevented Descartes from making a great discovery; and from this we conclude that behind many intellectual failures lies a failure of nerve.

Knowledge bureaucratized

A bureaucracy is a hierarchically organized institution whose purpose is to carry on certain limited functions. Thus a school system, the army, a university, the government, are all bureaucracies. It is common knowledge, however, that bureaucracies have three functions, rather than one. Although the first is ostensibly to carry out the tasks for which they are established, the definition of roles and the routinization of procedures in bureaucracies brings it about that an important function of the organization becomes that of preventing anything within it from changing. Even small change might make it necessary for the entire organization to change because each part is so interlocked with every other, that to alter any procedure in a bureaucracy without changing the rest is often like trying to increase the height of one wall of a house without modifying its entire configuration. A third function of a bureaucracy is to perpetuate itself, to prevent itself from disappearing. Given the functions of preventing internal change and struggling to survive, bureaucracies tend to devote much of their time to activities that will prevent change. Under these conditions it is difficult to introduce new knowledge into the system. Often only a general convulsion in the total society can compel a bureaucracy to change; and then it will do so only just enough to avoid going out of business. Obviously these are the conditions for incompetence: bureaucracies create the conditions for their own incompetence and hence for their own destruction. World convulsions have caused radical changes in the administration of the executive in our own government; the changes in the Department of Defense have been a response to world crisis; and the entrenched military brass have almost been swept away because they would not change. And so it goes. The feeling of vulnerability always creates efforts at defence but these very efforts only increase vulnerability over the long run because they cause incompetence. The feeling of vulnerability, efforts at defence by freezing the system, increased

vulnerability and ultimate destruction if there is no change –
this is the universal law of western civilization.

Competence for what and whom?

Anybody in our culture who suggested that we did not love our
children would be hated; and in harmony with our love of
children we want them to have the best education available. Of
course, it has to be the best education available for the money we
are willing to spend, and we all know that in calculating the
amount of money we are able – or rather, are willing – to spend
on education, the family standard of living comes first. That is to
say, after we have calculated expenditures for food, drink, enter-
tainment, the kind of clothes that will present us and our children
to the world in conformity with our class position, expenditures for fishing tackle, guns, high-fi sets, radios (several in one
house, TV (two or three in one house), outboard motor boats,
two cars, $30 to $40 dresses for the kid's graduation prom, two or
more bathing suits for everybody, a summer vacation, a barbecue
pit, a nice house with suitable mortgage and upkeep, hairdos,
mouthwashes, cosmetics, cigarettes, bowling, movies and repairs
on the car – I say, after we have calculated all these expenses –
not to mention taxes to state and federal governments – we are
willing to give our children the best education to be bought with
the money that's left over. Obviously not much is, and the continued defeat of one school bond issue after the other is witness
to the contradiction between educational goals and the living-
standard. Thus education, the very phenomenon that made a
rising living standard possible, is being undermined by it.

Another factor contributing heavily to incompetence in education is the war, for since taxes to support it draw heavily on all
of us, we are unwilling to be taxed for other things; that is to
say, we are unwilling to pay higher education taxes in the interests of our children. When we add the expenditures for the
spendthrift commitment to a good time and a rising standard
of living, our children get the dirty end of the stick. Let us put it
even more clearly: as far as education is concerned, war, a good
time and the living standard eat up so much that, in their education, the kids get the crumbs that fall from the table. Educational
crumbs can only be educational incompetence. On the other

hand, in a deeper sense, our children get the best education compatible with a society that requires a high level of stupidity in order to exist as it is. A moment's reflection will convince anyone that this is true. For example, if television had a truly well-educated audience and the newspapers and magazines well-educated readers, the economy would collapse because, since nobody would then be impressed by the advertising, they would not buy. Adults who had been trained by clear-headed, sharp-brained teachers would be imbued with such clarity of vision that they would not put up with many federal and local policies and they certainly would stop smoking. They might even begin to question the need for a standard of living that has spread wall-to-wall carpeting from here to California and given millions more space and more mobility than they can intelligently use. In the light of these terrifying possibilities the thought of an education in depth and sharpness for everybody can only make a thoughtful person anxious, because an education for stupidity is the only one we can afford right now.

I hope it is understood that no criticism is intended of socially necessary education for stupidity. Having been an educator much of my life, I understand that every civilization needs to introduce a reasonable amount of respectable intellectual sabotage into its educational system lest the young get out of hand and challenge or scorn tradition and accepted canons of truth. Too much striving by intellectual Samsons will only bring the temple down; it surely can do no lasting harm to cut their hair a wee bit. It looks better too: a crowd of crew-cuts or flat-tops looks so much neater than a mob of long-hairs. For a college teacher there is a certain comfort and tranquillity in dealing with students who have been trained in elementary and secondary school not to embarrass him by asking impertinent questions; and scarcely a day must pass when he does not give thanks to a system that has provided him with meek students who permit him to grow old without too much intellectual stir – without making him feel vulnerable.

Education and war

If we look at education and war from the standpoint of vulnerability, we see that in many ways education in this country today is hostage to our fear of communism; and revisions in the courses in maths and science are not going to help the child much, they are just going to make him better for the war machine and for the changing character of American industry which each day becomes more and more dependent on the sciences. Revision of the teaching of science and maths will not help the child much because we are not improving his skills in maths and science in the interest of his inner self but in the interest of war and business. Furthermore the overwhelming majority of girls will have no use for it and college students seem to show a declining interest in the sciences. The history of American education in the last hundred years, as set forth cogently by my colleague, Professor Callahan, shows that education has not considered the child's interest but that of industry; and I am not yet convinced that what is good for General Motors is good for our children. Even less am I convinced that what is good for Missile Dynamics is good for our children, or what is good for the Pentagon is good for them. Meanwhile the educational system, pressed by one world movement or local interest after the other, successively breeds one form of incompetence after the other. Each world hysteria generates a powerful group that sees itself as prophet of the system and the system yields to it. It is yield or die, because for the moment they hold overwhelming power.

It thus becomes clear that love of our children is, at best, qualified by our love of fun and the high-rising living standard, and that the Joneses, the McMullins, and the Schwartzes throughout the country do not love their children so much that they are willing to lower their living standard and give up some fun in the interest of raising the level of education to what is more in conformity with the possibilities of the richest and one of the most democratic countries in the world. It is also clear that, although we love our own children, it is not so clear that others – like business or the Pentagon – love them in the same way and for the same reasons.

Knowing our strength

I have spoken of the vulnerability – the susceptibility to destruction and defeat – of man in our culture. I pointed out that in order for society to continue it has to make us vulnerable – it has to create in us a vulnerable character structure, for did we not feel vulnerable society would have no way of making us toe the mark. I discussed Descartes because I wanted to show how what attacks all of us in the scholarly world – fear of punishment for making the very discoveries which are the goal and glory of our calling – prevented Descartes from discovering the calculus. Anyone who reads history and the social sciences critically learns that behind many intellectual failures is indeed a failure of nerve. The books we are compelled to give our students – largely because there are no better ones – are often boring and irritating, not because their authors lack brains but because they lack courage.

Thus it turns out that incompetence in education is in large part a consequence of fear – fear of one another and fear of communism}- and the case of Mrs Franklin is merely an extreme and overt expression of the widespread but covert process of sabotage that plagues the educational system and helps to make our children stupid. But the incompetence of the educational system is merely one form of bureaucratic incompetence, and all bureaucracies become incompetent because of fear.

The moral of all this is that we must know our strength. Nobody is invulnerable but nobody is as weak as he thinks he is either. Let everyone, instead of saying to himself, 'I am afraid,' say instead, 'I may be stronger than I think.'

2 Mental Health Problems in Elementary School

I went to school in New York's public schools; first to PS 10 and then to PS 186, Dewitt Clinton High School, and the College of the City of New York. When I went to primary school we had to sit up straight and were not permitted to utter a sound. We sat either with our hands behind our backs or folded on the desk in front of us. Those were the good old days, but I am quite tolerant of the contemporary system.

My paper is directed toward the problem of meeting the mental health needs of the child. Since this Institute enjoys the ambiguous title of the School's Role in Meeting the Mental Health Needs of the Child, and since there is nothing that happens to a child in school that does not have something to do with his mental health needs, the Institute's title gives one permission to talk about anything under the sun; for surely there is nothing in the school, from the number and position of the toilets and water fountains to the mental health of the teacher, the principal and the other students, not to mention that of the Board of Education, that does not have an impact on the mental health of the child. I shall, therefore, take up the challenge inherent in the title and shall roam among the various hazards. I am sure that after I have finished, you will perceive the obvious – that the greatest mental health need in the school is informed and mentally healthy adults, and that sometimes the sanest element in the school are the children, who fight to keep from drowning as the ocean of adult disorientation beats upon them. The simple fact of hazard has been obscured from the eyes of science because educators have been unwilling to inspect the products of their work; and for this reason the everyday, average, usual, run-of-the-mill transactions between teacher and pupil in the classroom have remained hidden from scientists, not to mention educators themselves, who are, of course, among the most unscientific professionals in the world. What I have to say, therefore, derives from many hunderds of hours of direct observation in nursery, elementary and secondary-school classrooms.

The process of formal schooling does not begin in the first grade, but for millions of children it begins in kindergarten, and for a smaller number in nursery schools, those ambiguous institutions which often have nothing of the nursery and still less of the school about them, and which, so far have enjoyed the same privileged secrecy as elementary and secondary-school classrooms.

Before discussing problems of the nursery school, it is necessary to present some theoretical considerations. The first deals with underlying assumptions about communication systems. Here we start with the axiom that every communication system is limited to certain types of signals. You cannot talk into a telegraph line or send teletype over radar or telephone systems. It is usually not possible to talk Chinese to a native American or to an American dog but you can talk English to both. A dog, however, will not understand the subjunctive mood, for its understanding is limited in general to certain simple forms of speech. You cannot talk existentialism to a child of two, although you can tell him to go to bed and expect him to understand it. Similarly, many signals emitted by two year olds are inaccessible to adults because the signals lack clarity for the adult. Thus, we make certain assumptions about a three year old's ability to understand. For example, it is certain he will not understand philosophy – that is, he will not be able to decode a message about, let us say, Heidegger. It is more certain, however, that he will be able to decode one about his breakfast. It is at this point that a fundamental problem arises in nursery school: what assumptions do we make about the nature of a child's communication capabilities? Such assumptions are important indeed for the cognitive fate of the child.

Let us proceed now to an examination of some actual communication between adult and child in a nursery school. We are present in a group of three year olds in a nursery school at 10.25 in the morning.

The teacher holds up an obviously brand new book titled *Snail, Where Are You?* She says, 'This is a listening book.' As several children start to speak at once, she says, 'Let's keep it a secret,' and holds her finger to her lips. She says, 'You will all have a turn but you must learn to keep it secret.' The book is almost entirely of pictures, beginning with a snail and going on to other objects, presumably having somewhat the shape of a snail: pigs' tails, a french horn, the horns of a mountain goat and so on. As the teacher turns the pages the children are chosen to take turns finding the snail. Most of the children are crowding close around the book, and after a short while few are sitting. There is some restlessness in competition for a turn. The teacher handled the group skilfully. She was gentle, never raised her voice and, since the book was a short one, was able to shift to a different activity just as things were disintegrating completely.

I first analyse the extract from the protocol into commonsense sections. First there is the presentation of the book as a 'listening book'. Next, the teacher, in an effort to control talking, says 'Let's keep it a secret.' Then there is the competitive crowding of the children around the teacher as they strive for a chance to find the snail in each picture, and finally there is the statement by the observers that the teacher 'handled the group skilfully and shifted to a new activity just as things were disintegrating completely'. I now examine the recorded transaction first in cognitive linguistic terms and then in reference to the observer judgement. I start with the emphasis on quiet indicated by the expressions 'secret' and 'listening book', and accompanied by the finger pressed to the lips, a further signal underscoring the importance of silence. Logical analysis of the use of 'let's keep it a secret' and 'you must learn to keep it a secret' provides the following sequence. 1. Secrets are silent. 2. The activity (of finding the snail in the picture) should be silent. 3. The activity, therefore, should be secret. That is to say the teacher has used the word secret in order to try to get the children to be quiet. What she has done is to use a word to apply to an activity where it has no place. Greater linguistic displacement occurs in the use of the expression 'this is a listening book'. Logically, this expression may be analysed as follows: 1. You must listen to what the other children say about the book. That is to say, listen to them pick out the snails. 2. This is, therefore, a book to be used by all the children while others listen to them. 3. Hence, this is a listening book. Hence the activity, listen, is transferred from the children to the book, so that instead of having a group of listening children, we have a listening book. I have elsewhere called this shift of activity from subject to object 'reversal of the actor' and also 'loss of the transitive sense'.* The use of this kind of language creates unnecessary cognitive hazards for children of this age. Considering the way they behaved they seem not to have had the faintest idea of what the teacher was talking about.

How does one account for this kind of language? It can be explained only in terms of assumptions made by the middle-class, white teacher about children. She has assumed that children understand best in terms of whimsey; that you enter the child's world through whimsey, and that the child will more readily obey if addressed in the language of whimsey, scrambled to taste by the adult. Thus the middle-class adult assumes that children of three readily decode whimsical messages because that is the way children think and that this is the best way to 'con' them into doing what you want them to do, as one of my students put it. You do this instead of issuing clear-cut commands. Every middle-class mother uses similar techniques. Thus, in this case whimsey is used in the interest of getting the kids to do what the white, middle-class adult assumes they will not do. The use of whimsey and distorted communication for related purposes is well known to us from advertising.

We must now ask: from whence comes the idea that children of three years can readily think of a book listening like a human being? Obviously from the unfounded assumption that children are inherently animistic, as if a tendency to view the universe animistically were genetically determined. Quite apart from the fundamental critical work by Margaret Mead † on this subject over thirty years ago, learning theory and comparative psychology should have by this time taught us that with the exception of a few basic drives and the enormous capacity to learn to perceive and to remember, practically everything a child has in its

* Jules Henry, *Culture Against Man*, Random House, 1963, ch. 8.

† Margaret Mead, 'An investigation of the thought of primitive children with special reference to animism', *Journal of the Royal Anthropological Society*.

head is learned. Since the only sources of social learning are adults and other children, the child must learn animistic notions from them. Mead has shown that the Manus, a tribe on a small island near New Guinea, are non-animistic as children but become animistic as adults. When our children talk with one another, however, at this age, they are usually very matter of fact; even when their play is imaginative, signals are clear. Our records of nursery school play show practically no animism or whimsical distortion of children's talk at this age. What we can say in summary then, is that adults often make unfounded assumptions about the way a child thinks and then act so as to force him eventually to actually think that way. This is reminiscent of the Jesuit missionaries in South America in the sixteenth and seventeenth centuries. Many of them had learned only one native language, Quechua, the language of the ruling clique of Peru; so when they later encountered Indians in the lowlands who knew nothing of Quechua, the missionaries taught them Quechua and proceeded to catechize them in that language. This forces upon us the shattering conclusion that since adults do not know the language of children and do not choose to learn it, they invent a language the children do not know and then force them to learn it. How could the poor little Indians resist?

I turn now to the observer's statement that the teacher handled the group skilfully and was able to shift to a different activity just as things were disintegrating completely. Since group disintegration is incompatible with skilful handling, the observer must be referring to the teacher's quietness and gentleness. But since quietness and gentleness did not prevent group disintegration, one concludes that these qualities have little to do with the management of this group of three year olds in a competitive situation. What is at issue here is the following: The observer is biased in regard to what constitutes good management. There is a dialectic opposition between mobilizing children's attitudes to a pitch of excitement and attempting to control them. This dialectical contradiction inheres in much of classroom management at levels above the nursery school and is a constant hazard in elementary school, where on the one hand an effort is made to relieve boredom by excitement, while on the other the children may be penalized for responding in the desired direction (of excitement). It is true that our culture relies on people's capacity to sustain a high pitch of excitement without breaking the bonds of propriety: football games and rallies, prize fights, violent movies and alcoholic flirtations are examples that come to mind. Nevertheless, we must be aware of what we are doing when we mobilize children's capacities for excitement in order to overcome their and our own boredom and in order to get them to do what we want them to do.

Characteristics of children's spontaneous speech

I have said that our records of hundreds of hours of observation of nursery schools at all income levels disclose no whimsey in children's conversations: that is to say, no distortion in which animateness is attributed to inanimate objects, in which the actor becomes the acted upon and in which attributes are irrelevantly displaced from one phenomenon to another. This does not mean that children are not imaginative, rather, that like the children's other faculties, their imagination is shaped by the culture. Of this we shall see more presently, but first it is necessary, in considering the nature of children from three to five years of age, to give some attention to serious errors in the understanding of the structure of a child's speech introduced into the literature of psychology by Jean Piaget, and according to which the language of children, even beyond the sixth year, is 'egocentric'.

When we consider that children from three to six play about us, under foot, in school, out on the playground and street and that they organize their play by speech, compare the properties of objects, scold and compliment each other, and so on, so that our ears are filled with their *social*, not egocentric, language, it is surprising that Piaget's theory has dominated child psychology for over a quarter of a century. It can only be because we think of our children as so troublesome and demanding that we regard them as egocentric, anomic, that is to say ruthless, inaccessible little monsters.

For illustrations of the practical, non-whimsical, though often imaginative, language of three-year-old children, I turn now to some selections from nursery-school play. I deal first with the play of the children involved in the listening book affair and then go to another school.

Dan has been painting his airplane made of two pieces of wood he has nailed together. Other children are sitting on the floor watching him. Dan says, 'Do you love it?' A boy, 'Is it going to be shined?' Dan, 'No, no, I am only painting it to make it pretty.' A girl says, 'Are you taking it home? Where are you going to put it?' A boy says, 'I know where you can put it, in your bathroom.' Dan says, 'In the basement.' Another girls says, 'Where are you going to hold it? Is it going to be an airplane?' Sometime later Dan is joined by David who has also made an airplane. He paints the plane reddish brown, working quickly and painting only on the top. David says, 'I am all finished.' Dan, pointing, 'You didn't paint it there.' David says, 'I don't have to if I don't want to.'

Examples of this direct speech could be multiplied. In the next example I show that even where the play context is imaginative, there is no distortion of speech. The example is from a different school and again the actors are three years old.

Five boys are in the doll corner. Doug, dressed in a skirt, is playing with a doll. Two boys are cooking, using realistic stainless steel pots and pans. Another boy says, 'There is a ghost in there.' He pulls the dress-up clothes off the shelves and dumps them in a pile on the floor, saying, 'These are poison. Look what I did to the ghost.' The other children ignore him. A boy who has left the group now runs back wearing a very realistic red plastic fireman's hat. He cries, 'Our house. It's burning, it's burning! Get out! Get Out! Mommy, Daddy, and Mailman!' The three children at the table immediately get up and leave the doll house. Their response to a play threat of fire is in marked contrast to the danger of a ghost. The boy who said he saw a ghost is left alone and he says to the observer, 'There was a ghost back there so I covered him up with the clothes.' He plays briefly at the stove and then runs back to the other end of the doll corner where the clothes are dumped on the floor and says, 'I got him! I got him!' Sybil is painting at the easel next to the doll corner. She looks at the observer and says reassuringly, 'There wasn't a real ghost.'

From these data one concludes that a fundamental mental health need of the child is adult understanding, unspoiled by misleading theory, of the cognitive processes of young children as they manifest themselves in social interactions and interaction with the real, though culturally determined world, of time, space, motion, objects, people and language. In order to achieve this, it is necessary to make a record of children functioning in their natural habitat.

I spent time discussing the nursery school in order to show why we must not assume that pre-school does not exist. Most children pass through some kind of kindergarten or nursery-school experience or both, so that by the time they enter the primary grades their minds have already had years of experience of the distortions and incorrect assumptions of the educational system. These are great mental health hazards indeed, for quite apart from purely emotional issues, cognitive problems play a critical role in mental health, and it is in the pre-school years that we can begin to see publicly what the cognitive hazards are. We can no longer pretend nursery school and kindergarten do not exist.

Some observations on elementary school

I turn now to the elementary school. Here, as in the pre-school environment, problems are innumerable and less known than the surface of the moon. We certainly must lay at the door of the schools of education responsibility for failure to study systematically the ongoing life of the schoolroom. In this paper I can discuss only a few of the problems that come to life when one studies classrooms by direct observation. I shall be concerned principally with problems of relatively common occurrence.

Attitude organization and readiness for triggering

I pointed out that three year olds in nursery school may become so excited by the activity in which the teachers induce them to engage that the group disintegrates. Let us examine a similar phenomenon in a third-grade classroom in a suburban school.

The children have been painting. The teacher says, 'Now listen to directions. We are going to have a contest. You will put the pieces of paper that are large enough to save on the table back by the puppet show and throw the scraps in the wastepaper basket. I'll see what group is finished first and sitting down facing front with their hands folded. Now begin.' There is much rushing, pushing, sliding, falling down. There is a big jam-up of children around the table, where they are supposed to put the paper that is to be saved. One girl just got a good kick in the shins and is beginning to cry. Another boy has been pushed to the floor. Observer remarks in her notes, 'I don't think this contest was such a good idea. I am afraid it is turning into mass confusion with a good possibility for someone to get hurt.' The record continues, everyone has returned to their seats. Teacher: 'This group could not have won because Steve and Judy made complete pests of themselves and added to the confusion. And this group,' she points to the two rows closest to the desk, 'could not have won because Bob did the same thing.' Teacher picks the middle group as the winner.

What has happened here is clear : the children were mobilized for maximal competitive strain and then penalized for straining. Some are physically hurt and others are humiliated by the teacher for trying too hard to do what she wanted them to do. The reward itself, recognition by the teacher for coming out first, is not worth that much anxiety and strain. This raises the whole question of striving. Can we be sure that even the winners in this contest do not ask themselves what it was all about? Can we be sure that this unnecessary competition and its problematic prize is not a paradigm for non-striving? That it is not laying a basis for the question, what am I fighting for anyway? The activity was converted into a competitive struggle engaged in for the teacher's benefit, not for the students', for the sole purpose of rushing things in this way was to get the room cleaned up in a hurry. Thus the children, mobilized to a fever pitch in the interest of the teacher, bowl each other over for a problematic reward, and suffer her reprimand into the bargain.

In the interest of getting the place cleaned up the teacher organizes the following attitudes she knows inhere in these middle-class American children : competitiveness, need for recognition, aggressiveness, desire to be speedy, tendency to admire orderliness. Thus she exploits these tendencies, organizing them to the point where the children fight to get cleaned up first.

Why doesn't this help the middle-class child lose faith in his own motivations? In American schoolchildren we observe a tendency to become feverish about almost anything they do that is not held under strict control. I call this tendency *readiness for triggering* and this readiness traps teachers so that they become angry, threatening and disciplining without knowing what has happened. In the next example I show this process at work in an apparently completely anxiety-free context; planning the menu for a school picnic.

The teacher says, 'Okay, what do you want to eat on your picnic?' Girls say potato salad. Teacher: 'We will take suggestions and then we will all choose.' Teacher writes potato salad on the board. Boys: 'Potato chips.' Teacher: 'Steve.' He says: 'Hot dogs.' Teacher: 'Let's not have any talking.' Other suggestions are marshmallows, hamburgers, fruit salad, soda pop. Teacher: 'We can't afford to buy soda for everyone for twenty-five cents.' Teacher calls on David. David says, 'Corn Kurls.' Everyone laughs. David says 'There are such things.' Child says, 'One of the mothers could make —' Teacher says, 'None of the mothers are going to make anything.' Kids call out, 'Fritos, cake, ice cream, candy!' Teacher says, 'Think before you suggest things.' Charlotte says, 'French fries.' Teacher says, 'Do you think that would be easy to make?' Then teacher says, 'Alright, stop talking. You are wasting our time. You may not talk, Charlie, until you raise your hand. You will have to learn that.' Kids call out, 'Relish, chocolate milk, grape juice.' Teacher says, 'Okay, Mary Lee. Jeff, we don't shout out.' Mary Lee says, 'Pork 'n beans.' Teacher says, 'Stop and think now if we have everything to make a well-balanced meal.' [Oral stimulation of this kind, getting children interested in food, really builds up very rapidly into a tremendous pitch of excitement. Nobody said steak or swordfish here but I've seen that happen in other circumstances. And, of course, when the kids think of food their imagination quickly takes possession of them. I remember one game of cafeteria in which children began to call out 'One hundred hamburgers,' 'One thousand steaks.' One scarcely knows, in a teaching situation, unless one has learned about these matters, how one particular thing will trigger the children, so that imagination takes complete control of their minds and bodies.] Now the teacher says, 'Charles don't talk out. You are going to have to stay after school if you don't stop.' She says, 'If you don't think we have everything for a well-balanced diet, raise your hand.' A child calls out, 'Cookies.' Another child says, 'We don't have enough vegetables.' And a boy shouts out 'Carrots and radishes.' Charlotte: 'Bread for the hot dogs.' Teacher: 'Yes, bread or buns.' Child: 'Some fruit.' Tanya says, 'Peanut butter and jelly sandwiches.' Teacher: 'Steve.' Steve: 'Can we have the kind of Corn Kurls that have a favour inside?' Everyone in the class laughs and teacher says, 'Corn Kurls is not a cereal, Steve.' Teacher is angry. She says, 'We have something else to do before recess. If you don't all be quiet, we won't have recess. Steve Smith get quiet. I don't think you are being a very good example. John, sit down. I am waiting for everyone to sit down and be quiet. If you don't, we will call this whole thing off.' [The teacher also threatens to shift to arithmetic.] Later a child asks the teacher whether they are really going to have the picnic or not.

Here we see the children's mounting excitement, the teacher's futile efforts to control it, the continuing and even more feverish excitement, the humiliation of some children, the final anger of the teacher, the threat to call off the picnic and shift to arithmetic. We all know how often arithmetic is used punitively, and we know that this is an excellent way to get children to detest it.

I believe the hectic behaviour could have been prevented in the two cases I have given by proceeding in an orderly way. After the art lesson the papers could have been picked up simply by asking the children to pick up those around their own desks and in the case of the menu the teacher could have asked each child in turn what he would suggest, or have had the children write down their ideas and hand them in. In both cases the striving for recognition, the excitement and the rewards and punishments emerged in striving for trivial goals. Thus we are profligate with the motivations of babies, wasting their motivations on nothing. I turn now to more desperate environments – those of the poor.

Schools with culturally deprived populations

Nowadays, education has another fancy word for poor children, we call them 'culturally deprived'. This has recently superseded the equally fancy term 'disadvantaged'. Yet it is clear to everyone who knows the families from which these children come, that they are deprived of everything – food, clothing, a wholesome family environment, and *hope*. When we consider, then, the milieu of these children, we wonder what has made us think that one woman could live with thirty or fifty such children in a classroom for five hours a day, day in and day out, no less teach them to read and write. It is common knowledge that classes of deprived children are often chaotic. We need, however, to have some direct observation of such schoolrooms in order to understand the dynamics. It is not enough to say that the teacher goes through hell. We need to know precisely what he or she goes through and what the children go through. We need to know more also about what strengths, what tendencies to order, yet remain to these children. For often when we expect things to completely fall apart the children pull themselves together and go on with their work. We need to know more about and to find ways of fostering this thrust toward health.

Hope, fear and organization

An ideal classroom is one in which all the students are participating in the lesson, but this can be obtained only through the school's ability to organize education-relevant attitudes that are in the students to begin with. It is common knowledge that in order for the school to be educational, there has to be something in the student that motivates him to education. Fundamental motivators are hope and fear: hope of achieving something and fear of punishment in case of failure to achieve. It follows that where neither hope of achievement nor fear of punishment for non-achievement are present, there is no motivation to education. Hope and fear organize human behaviour. We organize our lives because we hope to get somewhere; and education, that is to say information, is the fundamental organizer of behaviour. We work and strive because we fear to fail. When we study the way of life of poor Negroes, however, we find their life disorganized. Furniture is not only old, filthy and in scarce supply, it is often scattered in a disorderly way about the dwelling unit. Chairs and dirty rags may be on tables, and baby bottles on the floor. The gas stove may be lit when it should be off, and although the home may have more than one TV set, they may all be broken; and so it goes. Time schedules are of little account in homes where the head of the household is unemployed and where the windows look out on the vacant lot of hopelessness. Order is further broken down by fights and crowding. It seems typical middle-class lack of realism to say that the children coming from such an environment cannot cope with the organization imposed by schools. Yet, it must be said because it must be understood as a parameter in the confrontation between culturally deprived child and teacher.

The universe of participation

The word universe implies unity; yet children from disorganized backgrounds cannot create unity in the classroom; not only because for many reasons organization is difficult for them but also because the attitudes on which the school depends for its educational purpose are not present in many of the children. Under these circumstances the teacher as attitude organizer can work only with children who somehow have enough of the necessary attitudes to be organized by the school. We, therefore, sometimes see the harassed teacher working only with these children while letting the rest of the class carry on in a disorganized manner. Thus, the universe made up of those who participate in the classroom work becomes very small.

I now give some extracts from the record of observation of one such classroom. The teacher is a white female and the children are Negro and white. It is a sixth-grade class and the time is 11.00 a.m.

The teacher is leaning over Paul's desk helping him with arithmetic. Both her hands are on his desk. Paul is in his seat. His head is on one hand focusing on his paper. Irv and Mike are watching. Across the room Alice is talking to Jane and Joan to Edith. Behind me I can hear girls seated at the work-table whispering and talking. Nearby there is pushing and shoving in a group of boys, Alan, Ed and Tom. Tom gets out of his seat, makes a wad of notebook paper and tosses it in the air several times. He tries to catch it but drops it on the floor. As he bends to pick it up, he drops his pencil on the floor and kicks it four or five feet. He picks up the pencil and throws the wad at Alan. Alan turns to the observer, grins, waves his hand and says, 'Hi.' The teacher takes no notice. Tom and Ed suddenly slam their desks shut, get up and walk out noisily. As they leave, Lila and Alice hurry to catch up with them and walk out. Just before they leave the room, Tom turns and calls back to Lila saying, 'Come on, Lila.' A girl calls out, 'Good-bye.' And Josephine waves good-bye. With her back to the door, the teacher is talking to Jane. She stands by Jane's desk with her hands on it while they both look at the student's work. Irv gets up from his desk and walks over to stand near Joan's seat. Josephine gets up and pushes Irv and he pushes her. The teacher turns from Jane's desk, walks over to Josephine and Irv and steps between them. She flushes as she squeezes Irv's shoulder and pushes him away. Half-pushing and half-leading, she gets Irv back to his seat and forces him down into it. Josephine, very cocky, stands beside her desk, hands on hips. The teacher looks at Irv for a minute and then walks back toward the work-table. Irv sits at his desk but a minute and the next thing I know he is down on the floor. Mike and Paul are laughing at him and Mike seems to be kicking at him. Irv gets up and walks behind Mike's desk, clamps a head-lock on Mike and tries to pull him out of his desk. Mike is one of the kids that is working. The teacher walks back to the observer and says, 'Have you seen the poem on our bulletin board? I was so pleased with it. The pupils wrote it. They wrote it all. It is our first creative effort. I was happy to get it. We have all enjoyed it.' The bulletin board was neatly arranged. Paper three-dimensional figures illuminated the bulletin board and the words of the poem were written in black ink on white paper arranged step-wise across the bulletin board. It is now 11.12 a.m. [Everything here – and much omitted because of lack of space – has happened in twelve minutes.] The teacher is helping Mike. She stands beside his desk, looks down at his work but does not touch him. Lois has walked across the room to talk to John. Her voice is loud but the noise in the room is so great that it is difficult to her her. Lois and John leave the room, passing in front of the observer and saying, 'Excuse me.' The teacher goes to stand in front of her desk and announces that it is time to get ready to go. She puts on her coat, moves behind the desk, looks at the group, raises her voice to be heard, and says, 'While we are waiting for the bell to ring. . . .' Some hear her but others not. She stands, her arms folded, looking at the group. Some semblance of order seems to return. Irv and Mike are wrestling again and fall on the floor. The teacher looks at them. She appears impatient with them, for she is frowning. The boys take their seats looking sheepish but turn and giggle at each other. The teacher now touches the blackboard with her finger. On it are written the Latin words of '*Adeste Fidelis*'. I think that that is a Christmas carol that goes 'Come all ye faithful' but the words are in Latin. She says, 'Let's go over the words together.' The students say, 'We can't pronounce it. The words are too hard. We don't know it,' etc. To which the teacher replies, 'Well, we could do it all together. Come let's do it together.' A pupil says, 'I don't know those words.' He points. The teacher says, 'Well, I have gotten those two words mixed up too. They are *wenite* and *wedite*. Let's all say them together.' She pronounces the words and the class repeats them in chorus and they sing the song once more. The teacher seems to plead for attention, saying, 'We don't have much longer to wait. I know that you are uncomfortable but let's wait a little longer.' She looks at the class almost in desperation and says, 'Well, let's sing the song over again.' The children start singing.*

In this observation period, the only children who received instruction were Paul, Jane and Mike. The teacher let the other children do largely what they pleased while she gave herself to the three who were able to resist the general strain towards disorder and do their work. This phenomenon of *partial withdrawal* may occur under any circumstance where a single individual attempts to cope with a seriously disturbed environment. I have seen it in institutions for emotionally disturbed adults and children. The partial-withdrawal syndrome is not a function of the children or teacher only but involves also the dynamics of the total social situation. For example, in the selection just read, the children had a choice of seeking status with peers or with the teacher, for in this environment status with the teacher is viewed by some children as incompatible with status with peers. Here, most of the children abandon their lessons in favour of messing around with their peers. Such *self-destructive status choice* can be seen in varieties of disturbed environments, usually in environments where the choice is between a peer group and an authority figure; but especially where *hope does not tip the balance in favour of the teacher and self-preservation*. We see this sometimes in Negro children in integrated schools, where, in their anxiety to be accepted by the white children, the Negroes will follow the whites in messing around instead of yielding to the authority of the teacher. It is very likely that the seriousness of the problem of self-destructive status choice is increased when the disturbed situation has special attractions for the children. Thus, in a coeducational class the valence of the peer group is increased by sexual attraction, and in a bi-racial class, valence of peers may increase for the Negro children because of the attraction of the whites.

Every teacher knows that in school, and certainly up to the freshman year in college, there is a strain towards disorder, not towards homeostatis, in classrooms. When one studies the actual situation, whether in a family or in a classroom, one perceives

*The material reproduced here is used by courtesy of the Youth Project of the Greater Kansas City Mental Health Foundation.

that the concept of homeostasis is not applicable to social situations, and that we must take Cannon literally when he observes that what has to be explained about the body is its stability in the presence of enormous strains towards instability.

So far, I have attempted to identify some of the sources of strain in one schoolroom and explain the teacher's adaptation to them. I return now to the problem of the bulletin board in this class. One cannot but be struck by the disjunction between the disorder in the room and the teacher's calling the observer's attention to the bulletin board. One feels that turning away from the chaos of the class to the bulletin board is a form of disassociation – a shutting out of the noise and hurly-burly of the class. One wonders whether calling the attention of the observer to the bulletin board is not like saying, 'You see, we are not *all that* bad.' A common characteristic of adult functioning in an environment of disturbed and hostile children is a tendency to disassociate, to extricate oneself from the situation mentally if not physically. I have elsewhere called this 'delusional extrication'.* It is a way of denying that the phenomenon is there, and it is a way in which the adult can regain some composure. One sees this disassociation in dormitories for disturbed children, and it has been reported to me from schools for the Dakota Indian children where children may make a white teacher's life miserable.

Summary, conclusions and programme

We ought to begin our understanding of the mental health needs of the child the way Descartes began his understanding of the universe, by sweeping away everything of which we do not have a clear and distinct perception. Since education suffers from the fact that knowledge of the child is rudimentary and that knowledge of the social transactions of education is practically non-existent, it is bedevilled by untested assumptions about the cognitive, emotional, linquistic and imaginative processes of the child-in-school. The mental-health needs of the schoolchild are to be met, therefore, first, by investigating, with a mind free from preconceptions, the social process of learning as observable in nursery, elementary and high school. When this is done a new universe of knowledge opens to us, requiring new concepts. Thus

* In *Culture Against Man*, ch. 8.

in studying interaction between teachers and children in the nursery school, we discover adult linguistic distortions that seem to create real cognitive hazards for children. It seems that the particular distortions encountered in the example occurred, in part, as a function of the assumption that three-year-old children have to be trapped into doing what adults want them to. Another finding in the nursery school was that children's language, far from being whimsical and egocentric, is usually direct and social.

Turning to the elementary school, we saw that even when motivation is high, it may be used by teachers for trivial ends, and that the children may be punished for the expression of intense motivations that are mobilized by the teacher, who then punishes the intensity. In considering the experience of teacher and pupils in a school serving a deprived population, we saw that the teacher, in order to defend herself, may reduce the universe of participation to the tiny number of children able to take advantage of the educational opportunity. These are the survivors of an environment that is disorganized and hopeless. In such environments children may have no fear of failure because there is scarcely a criterion of success. In the disturbed classroom, we noted the following dynamics: the strain towards disorder; the partial-withdrawal syndrome; the self-destructive status choice; and the delusional extrication of the teacher.

In conclusion I propose the following. 1. Education of the deprived child should start from knowledge of the total environmental deprivation, including its cognitive and linguistic dimensions as well as its material and emotional ones. This cannot be obtained by interviewing but requires naturalistic study. 2. Before a deprived child is confronted with the formal materials of elementary school an effort should be made to constitute in him the frames of time, space, motion, objects, language, values and persons that have been destroyed in the deprived environment. 3. There must be in such schools a programme of total reconstruction for the deprived children starting with a breakfast that they and the teacher eat together. 4. For the deprived child education in the first three years should concentrate on the basic cultural frames; and other matters, such as music, art and crafts, should be postponed because these children, since they come from a disorganized environment, have such great difficulty in mastering the basic cultural frames. Finally, we know that if employment fails, everything fails. There is little use in talking about educating the child of poverty as long as he feels he has nothing to look forward to.

3 Hope, Delusion and Organization: Some Problems in the Motivation of Low Achievers

Since discussions of human motivation usually deal only in summary fashion with physiological motives, including survival, it is not possible to use current motivational theory when the context is one in which physiological motives, particularly survival itself, are paramount. This, however, is precisely the environment of many low achievers. Motivational theory includes the concept of goal, and uses such propulsive words as 'energizes', 'activates' and 'moves'. In the environments from which low achievers largely, though by no means exclusively, come, such ideas are hard to find. In reading about human motivation one is struck by the fact that what the motivation researchers have in mind, the hidden parameters of their thinking, are largely those attractive to the researchers. For example, in a recent book the following are stated to be 'secondary, learned, social, or psychogenic motives. . . . To strive for social acceptance or status, to work to write a symphony or climb a mountain, to try to keep the schools segregated or to integrate them, to want to complete college or understand human behaviour . . . saving for a trip abroad, working to get ahead, buying a new car or reading a book . . . heroism, martyrdom, artistic production or religious asceticism.'† While strictly speaking these are a mixture of ends and means rather than motives, the selection of examples illustrates the problem, viz., that the parameters of research in motivation are largely middle-class and elite; and from this point of view motivation is a unique psychological quirk characteristic of the middle and elite classes only. In such a context, then, most lower-class children could not be said to have any motivation.

We have been studying a housing development in a large city

*From *Department of Health, Education and Welfare Efficiency*, no. 31, 1965, pp. 7–16.
†Bernard Berelson and Gary Steiner, *Human Behavior*, Harcourt, Brace & World, 1964, pp. 240 and 241.

inhabited by very poor Negroes. One of the points brought out in our discussions of the tenants in the project is the tendency to random-like behaviour. Since we arrived at the notion of randomness through the impression that in their general conduct of life many of the households in the project did not conform to middle-class ways, we understand that the impression of randomness is relative – relative to middle-class behaviour. Bearing this in mind, we perceive that with regard to space, time, objects, persons and so on, the behaviour of the people who live in the project, failing to follow the patterns of organization characteristic of middle-class society, gives the impression of being random – i.e. lacking pattern and therefore lacking predictability from our (i.e. middle-class) point of view. The question arises, of course, whether the behaviour is random from their (i.e. dwellers in the Project) point of view. We have the impression, however, after seven months of fieldwork with about fifty families, that they look upon one another's behaviour in somewhat the same way. The distinction they make, for example between CP time (coloured people's time) and WP time (white people's time) is suggestive; for according to CP time one never knows whether an event will occur when scheduled, while according to WP time events scheduled for a given hour always occur at that hour.

The opposite of randomness is *organization*. The further down we go in the vertebrate phylum the more the organization of behaviour is determined by genetic mechanisms, although it seems that at no point is behaviour in the vertebrates determined exclusively by them. In *homo sapiens*, of course, it is difficult to show that any intraspecific (i.e. social) interaction is determined by innate mechanisms only; and the word *culture* has been chosen to designate what is determining in all the behaviour of *homo sapiens*. Yet *culture* has a certain phenomonology (i.e. a system of interrelated relatively standardized component perceptions) that is different for every culture; and this phenomonology exercises the same control over behaviour in *homo sapiens* that genetic mechanisms do in the lower vertebrates. We have a fairly accurate impression of what these component perceptions are in the middle classes and above in our society. The notions of achievement and security are familiar. We know also that these notions *organize* the behaviour of the middle class. The point of

view in which achievement and security are salient is comple-
mented by the opposites failure and insecurity. This logic enables
us to say that since achievement and security organize (i.e. make
non-random) the behaviour of the middle class their absence will
result in random-appearing behaviour. We may thus say that
wherever, in our culture, achievement and security cease to be
components of perception behaviour will appear random. This is
the condition in many households in the Project.

We have barely begun, however, analysis of the phenomonology of the culture of the middle class. We have yet to deal, for
example, with the problem of *hope*, *time* and the *self*. An important modality of achievement is *hope* and a central modality of
hope is *time*. Achievement has a temporal dimension, for it
means 'some time in the future'. Even when we say 'Billy no
longer wets the bed' we mean that *in the course of time* Billy
stopped wetting the bed, although he used to do it; and nearly
every parent hopes that his child will stop wetting the bed. We
can therefore imagine that the parent who has no hope has no
conception of his child's stopping wetting the bed. This behaviour in his child will therefore have dropped out of his conception of the *organization* of his child's behaviour. But in a
broader view, the person who has no hope of achievement or
security will have *no conception whatever of the organization of
behaviour* (relative to middle-class behaviour) at all. We can say,
perhaps, that the households of the project have no hope relative
to middle-class orientations and therefore their behaviour appears
random (i.e. unorganized) to a middle-class observer.

What then is the phenomonology of no hope? Though many
of the households of the Project have no hope, they nevertheless
wish to stay alive. Under these circumstances the *concrete factors
that keep them alive* (i.e. that save them from death) *move into
prominence*, and other perceptions (i.e. many perceptions
oriented toward middle-class organization) are not present in
awareness. What become salient are the factors that make a
direct contribution to *survival* : perceptions of objects, persons
and conditions that make a direct contribution to the *possibility
of death*, to the possibility of the *violation of the person* and to
the possibility of the violation of *material factors contributing to
survival*. In this context, the entire orientation toward objects

must change, for if objects do not contribute directly to survival, (to protection against death) they tend to become unimportant. For many dwellers in it, the Project is a culture oriented largely towards survival (towards *flight from death*). In this context disregard of many modalities of objects, for example, their arrangement in the house, becomes institutionalized, i.e. a way of life.

Let us now consider important conceptions borrowed from Heidegger.* When the middle-class person thinks about himself (or his self), he says, 'I *used* to be that way; here is the way I am *now*, and I *hope* I *will change* for the better.' These perceptions of the self have a past, a present, and a future; and from this middle-class view of self (*Dasein*) Heidegger derives our conception of time. Let us consider now the condition of people for whom this comparison does not exist, i.e. people who do not view the self as in a state of change. Obviously if the self is perceived as in a state of change from what *used to be* to a state of what *hopefully will be*, a certain organization of activity must ensue; for the passage consciously and determinedly from what used to be or what is now to a state of what will be requires an organization of existence that will bring these changes in the self to pass. But if this temporal modality of the self drops out the organization in the activities of the middle-class, self will not appear. Hence, having no perception of temporal dimensions of the self, the behaviour of such a person appears unorganized, i.e. random. What remains is the *survival self*, the self that is in flight from death. This self then becomes preoccupied with activities that give it *the most intense sensation of being alive*; it is a self that has, at every moment, to literally feel its life. This is the condition the middle-class sociologists contemptuously call 'hedonism'. But it is not hedonism; it is merely flight from death.

It may be helpful now to look at the apparently random behaviour of the dwellers in the Project in the metaphorical context of entropy. In thermodynamics entropy is a measure of randomness and hence of loss of organization. We can say, therefore,

* Martin Heidegger, *Being and Time*, Harper & Row, 1962. Heidegger, of course, has no interest in culture and even less in social class. The discussion merely borrows some of his fundamental conception of *Dasein* as a temporal being.

metaphorically speaking, that entropy is maximized in many households in the Project. In thermodynamic theory, however, entropy increases in closed systems only; that is, in systems that cannot receive energy from outside the system. The isolated quartz crystal is a common example. Before attempting to view the Project (metaphorically) as a closed system, let us look at its opposite, a middle-class dwelling area. There we perceive that the members have relatively free access to the major sources of cultural (including economic) stimulation and therefore households are able to maintain organization (entropy is at a very low level). In the project, however, the households do not have available such sources. And here is the paradox, for what prevents the dwellers in the Project from having access to the major sources of cultural stimulation is their randomness, and absence of hope, and what created randomness and lack of hope in the first place was inaccessibility of the cultural resources. We can therefore say that since the households of the Project are alienated from middle-class culture, their entropy can only increase.

It goes without saying, of course, that the self of many among the middle class is also in flight from death, but since in the middle class the orientation towards achievement is the lens through which existence is perceived, and since they have been taught the possibility of hope, they *fly from death towards achievement*, sustained by hope. This way of seeing life and this way of being sustained are not available to many of the dwellers in the Project – to many dwellers in the slum.

We thus come to the realization that hope is a *bounding* phenomenon; in the sense that hope separates the free from the slaves, the middle and upper classes from much of the lower class, the hopeful from the hopeless. We thus come to an even more unexpected conclusion, to wit, that time, space and objects exist in an environment of hope.

The delusional system

Since the Project is isolated from the main stream of social and economic life of the city as well as from the white community, the occupational classes of the census bureau do not apply to the tenants. Since most of the people work at interstitial jobs or as domestics, and employment is precarious and poorly paid,

resources are scarce. Though the Project is almost literally a
'City of Women', for a very large number of husbands are tran-
sients or have deserted, we find women talking about husbands
as if they existed, and we find unemployed men talking as if they
had jobs. In addition there is the constant effort to build one's
self up, by inflating one's self, by spending one's money on very
expensive clothes and by getting the better of another person.
Thus achievement is delusional also. In view of this one can
understand the remark of a white schoolteacher working with
poor Negro children, that they are not interested in solid accomplishment but rather in showing off. All of this must interfere
with learning in school or even taking school seriously. Thus we
see that just as violent rejection by a parent tends to create delusional fantasies in his children, the casting out of the Negroes by
white society results in the development of a social life so saturated with delusion that *delusional* achievement becomes the *real*
achievement.

Summary and conclusions

In attempting to examine the achievement problem in very,
very poor Negro children, I suggest that they lack both
hope of achievement and fear of not achieving and that they
come from a culture lacking characteristics of order fundamental
to the achieving middle-class culture. Specifically their homes
are physically and personally disorganized; life does not run on
a time schedule and so on. Thus, emotionally and cognitively
they lack the structure on which a conventional educational
system can build. When thirty to fifty such children are placed
in a classroom run by one teacher, the result is bound to be a
disorganization, from which the teacher will select those elements of order suited to her task: she will teach the children
who are teachable and let everybody else go. Meanwhile, even the
children who want to learn are under tremendous pressure from
their peers to give up. Thus the motivation of the low achiever
is not a demon locked up inside of the child, but is at every
moment, especially in school, subject to manipulation by the
peer group as well as by the teacher. One might urge, therefore,
that in considering improving the motivation of the child one
should also improve the school as a social system.

Proposals
A programme of total reconstitution

Filling the cognitive gap. I have pointed out that because of the disorganization of the environment the basic perceptual frames of these children do not seem to have been properly constituted: houses and people are in a constant state of disorder and things do not run on time. Yet these children are supposed to master mathematics, the central idea of which is order. I would urge that in pre-school these children be formally introduced to fundamental shapes and categories: insidedness and outsidedness, roundness, straightness, flexibility, rigidity, transparence, opaqueness, motion in a straight line, in a circle, rocking motion, motion that rolls but moves in a straight line (like an automobile, for example). Problems in the articulation of gears and movement in several planes at once (as, for example, in a manually operated egg-beater). Things that flow (water and sand – as in and out of a sand pail), things that 'shove along' (like blocks), and so on. Through planning basic experimental frames much can be done in building up the necessary perceptual competence in these children prior to their entrance into elementary school.

Emotional calming down. These children often come to school unfed after wretched nights torn by screaming, fighting, bed-wetting, etc.; often they cannot sleep because of cold and rats. For such children to start at once the routine work of the average elementary school class is impossible, for not only are they hungry and sleepy, they are emotionally upset. It is therefore proposed that teachers be trained to deal with the problems of these children, and that such trained teachers have breakfast with the children in school. It is expected that the school will furnish the food. Of course, one does not have to wait until the teachers are trained in order to bring children and teachers together at breakfast. The purpose of the breakfast is twofold: 1. To feed hungry children; 2. To bring teacher and pupil together in an informal atmosphere before the pupils are placed under the strain of classroom constriction.* *It is essential that the teacher be present,* so

---

* One such programme in Kansas City worked an immediate sharp improvement in attendance and all other areas of behaviour as well as in schoolwork.

that the students meet her under the calming conditions of friendly eating together.

Under these circumstances the personalities (the 'egos') of the children, badly battered by their night's ordeal, will be 'reconstituted'. The more the teachers know about the emotional management of these children, of course, the better.

Expansion of the universe of participation

This may be done either by reducing the size of the classes or by increasing the number of teachers in the classrooms to two or three. These have to be trained personnel, who know the subject matter of the lessons. The supernumerary personnel could be teachers-in-training, members of the domestic Peace Corps – whoever is in a position to learn the material.

4 Education of the Negro Child*

The education of the deprived child is now associated with the names of many workers.† All of their studies are of groups of children and most of them rely on test materials. Many emphasize the effects of language and usually stress the absence, in the life of the culturally deprived child, of a variety of cognitive experiences and material conditions not present in the life of other children. The conclusions all point in the same direction – that the culturally deprived child starts school with initial handicaps that make failure almost a foregone conclusion. Since, in spite of the evidence for the low probability of educational success of the deprived child, we know that some succeed, it is necessary to find out why they do in order that we can make more of them succeed. The only way to find out is to study individual children; and one of the best ways to do this is by a natural history method, in which research focuses not on groups but on particular children followed through their educational experience for a length of time manageable by the usual strategies of investigation.

In this paper I report on a very small pilot project in the natural history of the education of two Negro ghetto children from kindergarten through the first grade.

Objectives

The purpose of this project is to study the natural history of the education of the poor Negro child. The natural history of the

*Prepared during the author's tenure as Fellow at the Center for Advanced Study in the Behavioral Sciences, Stanford, California. The material on which this paper is based was collected by Miss Gwendolyn Jones, as part of a study of a de facto segregated Housing Project in a large city.

† A few references directly relevant to this chapter are contained in the bibliography on p. 69. For an excellent review of the field, as well as mas-

education of a child is a description of the learning experiences of a child in its natural habitat. The question is: what is the habitat? What is a learning experience? Over how long a period is the history to be studied?

The child's habitat is home, school and areas frequented by the child outside the home, together with the people in them.

For the purpose of this project education is defined as *all* the experiences of a child, because in all contacts with the external world the child may learn something. Under such a definition being beaten, hearing one's confused great-grandmother-care-taker be gulled by a sewing machine salesman or miscount a dozen-and-a-half eggs are just as much learning experiences as sitting through a reading lesson in school. It can be seen, especially from the example of the confused great-grandmother, that in humans there is both positive and negative learning; positive learning being learning congruent with dominant cultural conventions (including cognitive systems) and negative learning being learning not congruent with such systems. It can be seen from the above examples that 'negative' is not synonymous with 'aversive'. One hypothesis of this study is that much more learning is negative among the poor than among other classes.

The natural history of a single organism covers its life; but this study will be limited to the child's learning experiences in kindergarten, in the first year in elementary school and in his home peer-group during that period.

The rationale for a natural history of the education of any child is that by studying the *same* child over a wide range of his activities we get a more complete idea of what helps *him* and hinders *him* in learning. When the *same* child is studied for two years in the home, in kindergarten, in the first grade and with peers, one obtains a better picture than when one studies him in only one of these situations. Furthermore, by following *specific* children over time, one obtains a more detailed and faithful picture of the vicissitudes of the educational experience of particular children than when one studies *groups* at a *single moment* in time, without reference to the question of the varieties of

---

sive bibliographic materials on deprivation and education, the reader is referred to Joe L. Frost and Glenn R. Hawkes (eds.), *The Disadvantaged Child*, Houghton Mifflin, 1966.

experience *over time* of each particular child. Thus in this study we aim at the significant detail of life experience of *particular* children rather than at global statistical formulations based on *group* studies. We think that the study of the natural history of selected children will enable us to articulate, or, at least, to approximately articulate, the varieties of experience with one another. From the work of Deutsch, Riessman, Bruner and others we have been made aware of the probable relationship between milieu (home and peer) and school learning in culturally deprived children; we want to be able to specify that relationship in greater detail and with security.

There are factors in the home that are as important to school performance as cognitive capabilities and reinforcements narrowly construed. We refer to factors generally called emotional. The cases of two poor Negro children, David Smith and Rachel Potter, cast light on the issue.

David and Rachel

David and Rachel are described by the researcher as outgoing and alert when first observed in kindergarten in 1964. Now both are in Mrs Trask's first-grade class. Both children live in the same Public Housing Project. Rachel's building has no bad odour, the halls in David's smell of urine. Rachel's family is stable 'middle-class-like', David's is not.*

Rachel

Rachel is one of five children and lives with her father and mother. Father, an unskilled worker, is a family man, but seems rather aloof from the children. Mrs Potter was observed to be always deeply involved in them.

The Potter's apartment has four rooms: a combination living-room and kitchen-dining area and three bedrooms. The apartment is always neat and the furniture is so arranged as to make a clear distinction between living-room and dining-kitchen areas. The front area presents the family 'front' but the rear rooms are drab and bare. The children all have permanent bedroom assignments. Only members of the nuclear family live in the apartment.

* It is well known, of course, that ghetto Negroes are not a homogeneous class.

Mrs Potter seems affectionate with the children though firm. She is always clear-headed. She is active in a religious movement, there is literature of the movement around the house, and the family has study periods devoted to the ideology of the movement.

The Potter children are very competitive with one another but are obedient to maternal intervention, which is generally in the interest of maintaining proper conduct: 'Give Pam a chance, Rachel, it's not your turn.' The children often play at schoolwork and TV-watching seems to be subordinated to it.

David

David's household is held together by his illiterate fifty-nine-year-old great-grandmother Mrs Thompson. The following persons seem to live there at present with some continuity: David and his four sisters; his violent (diagnosed), psychopathic but probably borderline psychotic, thirty-five-year-old great uncle James, son of Mrs Thompson; Mrs Thompson's fifteen-year-old 'daughter' Josephine;* and Thomas, a grandchild of Mrs Thompson. David's mother and father are separated and neither lives in the apartment. Marilyn, the mother, characterized as 'wild' by Mrs Thompson, is irregularly resident in the home, as is Sandra, another daughter of Mrs Thompson.

The apartment has the same physical layout as the Potters' but is always in disarray, furniture is moved around frequently and no clear distinction is maintained between living-room and kitchen-dining areas. The only person who has a fixed sleeping place is James.

Mrs Thompson is almost entirely dependent on public agencies. A D C checks go to Marilyn (David's mother) but none of it has been used to support the children.

Mrs Thompson says she could not live without the children. Observation indicates she is well-disposed towards them but her contacts with them are rather impersonal. In speaking about them, in their presence she often belittles them and herself as well. She has had a stroke, her eyes are bad and she is quite confused but far from mentally ill. She is unable to discipline the

---

*The Housing Project has not been able to verify Mrs Thompson's claim that Josephine is her daughter.

children and has little authority or respect in the house. Mrs Thompson's communication with the children is limited largely to commands and admonitions. In general, it is infrequent. David and his siblings interact competitively but most time at home is spent watching TV. The children were never seen to do schoolwork at home. James is a punitive and threatening figure.

Observation in Rachel's home

Both Mr and Mrs Potter are stable figures in the lives of their children. Mrs Potter has frequent, intimate and affectionate contact with them. The father is absent from the house during work and watches TV in the evening. Mrs Potter is a housewife and Mr Potter is definitely a 'family man'. There is a very warm relationship between Mrs Potter and her children, and she appears sure of her position as an authority and as a nurturant figure. Rachel spontaneously includes her mother in her play.

[Rachel and several playmates are jumping rope.] R: 'Mama, let me see you jump rope.' Mrs Potter smiled, said OK, and jumped rope.

[Rachel and several of her friends are playing school.] Mrs Potter looked over at the kids, saw that Rachel was holding all the pencils. Mrs Potter asked Rachel why she had all the pencils and Rachel replied that the other kids weren't supposed to be doing anything now. Mrs Potter told her to give the children their pencils and Rachel repeated that they weren't supposed to be doing anything now. Her mother then told Rachel to give them their pencils. 'Now – give Betty her pencil.' Rachel sat pouting for a couple of seconds, and her mother said, 'Give it to her!' and Rachel took one of the pencils and threw it to Betty who picked it up. Mrs Potter told Betty to put the pencil back down and for Rachel to give it to her. Betty did, and Rachel handed her the pencil. She then gave Alice and Jennie their pencils back. Rachel immediately turned her paper over and told the kids what to draw.

The kids were still playing school and Rachel now was just sitting and watching the other kids as they worked and Mrs Potter said, 'Look at Rachel. Rachel is lazy.' And Rachel said, 'I ain't. I ain't lazy either.' And Mrs Potter said, 'You just have one thing to do and that's wipe off the table, and you don't do that well today.' And Rachel kind of grinned when she said this.

We continued watching the children and every once in a while Rachel would ask her mother something related to the work she

(Rachel) was doing, or her mother would comment. At one point Rachel said, 'I'm going to make six mice with cheese,' and her mother said, 'Mice with cheese. Show me how you draw that, Rachel.' And Rachel began. When she finished she went to show her mother.

Rachel was telling the other kids that, 'When I finish this you're going to have to draw it,' and her mother said, 'They're going to have to draw it, but you didn't draw that. Alice drew that.' And Rachel said, 'I know it, but I'm the teacher. They're supposed to do what I say.'

These data show that there is a high level of verbal interchange between Rachel and her mother, that the mother intervenes constantly in Rachel's play and will participate in it if asked. Mrs Potter's intervention is in the framework of positive learning: she teaches Rachel the right thing to do – not to be selfish, to give other children a chance (fair play), not to try to run things. She intervenes in the interest of moral learning and justice. Her intervention is non-violent and she does not threaten Rachel with beating. There is an easy interchange between Rachel and her mother and she brings her mother her work to see as if she knows her mother will be interested.

Observation in David's home

David's home is usually in a state of disarray, while Rachel's is always orderly. The different arrangement of furniture in the two apartments is illustrative. The furniture in David's house is usually covered with an assortment of articles; outstanding are the persistent piles of clothes that Mrs Thompson is to iron.

The observer [R] asks: 'Whose room is this? Who sleeps here?' Mrs Thompson: 'Room? Whose room? Oh well, I guess it's Josephine's room. I guess she's supposed to sleep here, but you never can tell. The kids just sleep all over. You never know who's going to sleep where. Sometimes I have a hard time finding a place for myself.' R. 'Oh, the kids don't have any special place they have to sleep?' Mrs Thompson: 'No, they just sleep anywhere they want.'

We then watched television and there was very little comment during the programme except for the kids laughing at some of the antics or jokes. When this programme went off, 'Petticoat Junction' came on and we watched it. During this programme, David was sitting over on the bed also. Lila went over to where Mary was and tried to get her to move over so she could sit there too and Mary hit Lila saying, 'Go away, move.' The girls started hitting each other. Mrs Thompson: 'You all stop that. You all cut that out. Tillie, give me my switch, give me my belt over there.' Both girls were crying by this time and Tillie looked in a drawer and came out with what seemed to be a plastic-covered extension cord, or a clothes line. It was looped several times over and she gave it to Mrs Thompson who shook it at them saying, 'You all hush up that noise, you just hush up that fuss,' and she sat back down. Lila hit at Mary again. Mrs Thompson: 'I told you about that,' and she got up, and with both hands hit Lila on the ears several times, saying, 'I told you to stop that.' Lila started to cry and Mrs Thompson said, 'Go on in there and clear up them dishes.' On the table, where apparently someone had been eating, were three plates with a lot of bones on them. They looked as if they may have been pig knuckles or pig feet bones. Mrs Thompson: 'Go on in there and start them dishes.' Tillie went also and after a few minutes David went too. R: 'Where is Josephine tonight?' Mrs Thompson: 'Oh, I don't know. I don't know. I'll probably have to send these kids out to her again. I just don't know what I'm going to do with that girl.'

It will certainly strike middle-class readers as strange that nobody should have a permanent sleeping place in this home; but when one considers that in this, as in many ghetto homes, the population of the household is in constant flux, and that each new person (in the sense of new arrival or of a former inhabitant returning) may require new adaptations, it makes sense not to insist on rigid sleeping arrangements. Nevertheless, having a fixed space gives the child a certain advantage in school learning over a child who is strange to such stability.

Note that there is no play and verbal communication is low. The observer never saw any schoolwork being done in David's home, not even in play. Note also how quickly Mrs Thompson moves from admonition to extreme violence. Readers not familiar with ghetto culture may not understand the significance of the plastic-covered extension cord: in some ghetto homes the cord is used to beat children, apparently because blows with the hand are so common that they lose effectiveness. At any rate, it is clear that Mrs Thompson comes to feel very quickly that the situation is beyond her unless she uses violence. Note that as soon as the fighting blew over and the children were ordered to clean up the kitchen, all verbal interchange ceased.

The answer to the question about Josephine is relevant to ghetto life: Josephine is fifteen years old and probably already deep in the ghetto female sexual cycle.* Note that Mrs Thompson feels helpless and that she objects to what Josephine is doing, even though she must know that such behaviour is typical. Rejection of the ghetto female sex pattern in judgement, but accepting it eventually as a fact, is characteristic.

The next observation is of James and David. James, arrested because of violence to one of his sisters and for having smashed Mrs Thompson's furniture, has been diagnosed as 'psychopathic personality'. The observation follows.

James entered the room and said to Miss Jones, the researcher, 'You David's teacher? You taking him somewhere?' And [Miss Jones continued] I said, 'No, I'm not a teacher but I'm going to take him out today.' Tillie [a sister] said, 'Granma said he could go. She said he's supposed to go.' James grabbed David, put his arms around him, and all of a sudden slapped him hard on the head. I guess I must have shown some obvious signs of shock because James then rubbed David's head and said, 'He knows I'm not mad at him. He knows the difference between my hitting him when I'm not mad and when I'm mad.'† I gave a kind of half-hearted smile, nodded my head, and sat down. When we left, James was careful to pin up David's coat.

In the summer of 1965 David 'took to running away,' says Mrs Thompson, 'with a group of them little bad boys around here.' Sometimes he wouldn't come home until two or three o'clock in the morning. People who knew him would report seeing him all over the place. Once he went all the way down to the river. At her wits' end, Mrs Thompson got somebody to round up David's father, in the hope that he could stop the child from running away. Though David's father shows no interest in him, is not living with David's mother and never appeared in the home, he did come in answer to this summons and, Mrs Thomp-

---

* See Lee Rainwater, 'The Negro family, crucible of identity', *Daedalus*, Winter 1966.

† I'm not at all sure that this very good Queen's English isn't Miss Jones's modification.

son said, 'When he brought David back he beat the living day-
lights out of him. He beat the boy hard for an hour; he just took
off his belt and just wore him out.'

When Miss Jones was still getting to know the family, she
paid a visit one day, and David, whom she already knew quite
well, was called into the room by Mrs Thompson, but was quite
shy in responding to Miss Jones:

Mrs Thompson sat down in the armchair by the window and asked
me [Miss Jones] if I thought something was wrong with David, if
maybe he couldn't learn. She said she tried and tried to get him
to speak up and to say something but he just won't. She said she
tried to get him in every programme at school and then she corrected
herself and said in all the programmes at church. She said that there's
going to be an Easter programme and that there was a real good
part in it and David was supposed to be in it but he won't say anything. He'll just get up there and mumble and you just can't understand him. She asked me again if I thought there was something
wrong with him, that he couldn't learn. I told her I was sure there
wasn't. I then asked her what church they attend and she said, 'The
People's Church.' She said that 'David just acts so dumb at times.'

Mrs Thompson belittles the other children, and herself. Thus
David does not get anything at home which makes him feel intelligent. Observed in kindergarten with his peers at their desks, David
is very talkative. When Miss Jones brought him and Rachel to the
university to visit me he talked a blue streak, and coherently.

In the next excerpt from Miss Jones' observations we get a
good picture of Mrs Thompson's confusion and the lack of respect for her by other adults that come to the house. The reader
should recall that Mrs Thompson is illiterate and cannot see
well. The Project had been trying to get her to an eye clinic for
some time, but in June 1966, we had not yet succeeded, even
though we were going to pay the fare and the cost of the glasses.

I [Miss Jones] entered the apartment and sitting on the right-hand
side of the table was a white man. On the table was a new portable
Singer sewing machine. Mrs Thompson sat down and said that she
just wasn't too well, that she had just gotten back from downtown
(on a table and chair where the sofa had previously been were a lot
of packages) and that that girl (her fifteen-year-old niece) had just
talked her out of spending every penny in her pocketbook. She shook

her head and said she just didn't know why she had done it, she just didn't know. I asked who she was referring to and she said that she was talking about that big girl that had been there when I was there before. She told me that she had said that she wasn't going to buy that girl anything for Easter because she had been disobeying her for about the past three weeks but somehow or other she had talked her downtown and just talked her out of all her money and buying her a new dress, pocketbook, shoes and just everything. She kept repeating that she just didn't know why she had done it. She then asked me if I thought maybe she was losing her mind and I said that these things happen to a lot of people. She shook her head again and repeated that she had said she wasn't going to buy that girl anything. She then said, 'Someone must have sprinkled some gooby dust on her.' . . .

The white man looked in his pocket for something or other and stood up and began talking to Mrs Thompson about this new sewing machine on the table. I think they were continuing the conversation I had interrupted when I arrived. Mrs Thompson told me that she would have to give him the $12 next week and that she guessed he'd take the new machine back and she'd keep her old machine until she had the money and the salesman then said it was supposed to be $20, that she had already given him $8 so she could keep the new machine and he'd just pick up the money next week. She said no, she guessed he'd better take the new machine on back until next week because you're supposed to have the $20. The salesman then explained that the $20 had already been paid to the company, that he had taken the $8 she had given him and put the other $12 in from his own pocket and given it to the company; so the $12 she would give him next week would be his, and the company had its money for the machine. . . .

The salesman went and brought in what was apparently Mrs Thompson's old machine. He sat it down and Mrs Thompson said, 'You don't reckon I've got $50 in that, do you?' He said, 'I beg your pardon.' She said, 'You don't reckon I've got $50 in that?' He asked if she meant that the machine wasn't worth $50, and she said, 'I didn't think so but look in the drawer.' She looked in the drawer and started taking some pins out. The salesman said that he had taken everything else out of the drawer and put it on the table back there. (I am unclear myself as to whether Mrs Thompson was wondering if the machine was worth $50 or if she had $50 in the drawer of the machine.) . . .

Almost as soon as he had left the apartment, Mrs Thompson's

daughter Sandra, a woman in her middle or early thirties who looked as if she were about seven months pregnant, entered the room. She was wearing a red and white striped maternity top and Jamaica pants. She was wearing a wedding ring. Sandra picked a cloth bag off the table that had the Singer emblem on it and said, 'What this go to? I could sure use this. I could use this.' And Mrs Thompson said, 'Put that down, Sandra, that's to my machine.' The girl said, 'I could sure use this; aw, it's not important.' The salesman then re-entered the apartment and looked around and Mrs Thompson said, 'Sandra, get up and let the man have that seat.' The girl said, 'I'll get up when Sandra's ready to go.' The man said, 'Oh, that's all right,' and he opened his attaché case on the floor and took some papers out of it. While he was doing this, Sandra looked at him and said, 'You don't want this seat, do you?' And he said, 'No.' Mrs Thompson said, 'Give the man the chair.' Sandra said, 'I done ask if he wanted it and he said no.' She was still holding the cloth bag and Mrs Thompson asked the salesman, 'Is that bag mine? Does that bag go to the machine? What's it for?' He said, 'It's to cover the foot pedal with, to hold the foot pedal when you aren't using it.' She said, 'Put that down, Sandra, it's mine.' And Sandra said, 'You don't need this. It'll be on the floor more than anywhere else anyway.'

Mrs Thompson then told the salesman, 'I don't know, maybe I should keep my old machine this week. I made two dresses already but I've got three more Easter dresses to make tonight.' (On a pole lamp by the sofa two new dresses were hung. In all probability these are the dresses Mrs Thompson has already completed.) The salesman said, 'It's easy to use this machine. You'll be able to sew so much better with it.' Mrs Thompson then said, 'But I don't know if I know how to work it and I got these three dresses to make. Maybe I should use my old machine to finish those dresses.' The salesman said, 'Here's the book and do you want me to show you how to use it again? I'll show you.' Mrs Thompson: 'Not right now. I still think I ought to keep my old machine now, even if it is old. I've had it twenty years, let me see ... yeah, been twenty years and I don't know if I can change now. It doesn't act right sometimes and it skips stitches at times but I know how to use it. I'm used to it.' She then asked me, 'Don't you think I'm too old to learn this new machine, these new things now?' And I said, 'Oh, I don't know about that.' And Mrs Thompson said, 'I don't know, I'm too old to be getting into all of this debt. I'm paying $400 for that machine.'

By this time Sandra had gone into the kitchen area and was putting something in a paper bag and she said, 'Hmmp, this one's cracked,' and laid an egg to one side. Mrs Thompson: 'Those are hard-boiled eggs.' Sandra: 'No they ain't. I just took these out of the refrigerator.' Mrs Thompson: 'Oh, how many eggs you taking, Sandra? I know you taking a dozen and a half. I know twelve's in a dozen and a half a dozen would be about six more. You ain't fooling me; I know you taking more than a dozen.' Sandra: (who in the meantime keeps putting eggs in the bag) 'Aw mama, you don't know.' Mrs Thompson: 'Sandra, don't take all of my eggs!' Sandra: (looking in the bag) 'Aw, I'm just taking a dozen and one in case one of 'em breaks so I'll have an even dozen. I just took fourteen, maybe sixteen or eighteen.' then she stops taking eggs and puts the bag to one side. The salesman has left the apartment again, I guess to go back to the car for something. Sandra then goes over to the piano and begins playing something. Mrs Thompson: 'Sandra, don't play the piano, it makes me nervous. I can't take it today.' And Sandra keeps on playing and says, 'Aw it's not long.' Mrs Thompson: 'Sandra, don't play the piano, it's making me nervous I say.' Sandra: (finishes what she was playing) 'I don't know but one number anyway.'

The following points should be stressed in connection with these observations: 1. Mrs Thompson's general confusion and inability to make a decision and stick to it; 2. the ease with which adults, coloured or white, push her around; 3. the chicanery of the white salesman, who insists on selling Mrs Thompson a sewing machine when she obviously will not be able to run it and when she is obviously confused about costs, and about her ability to pay for it; and 4. the lack of respect for her by members of her own family. Thus David does not have before him models of adults who are honest or solicitous; and the major adult influence in his life, his great-grandmother, does not provide him with any firm basis for making a decision. In sum, David's home environment lacks important dimensions that usually give firmness to life, including perception and cognition.

The following suggests a further source of confusion and even despair.

Mrs Thompson began crying and said, 'I just don't know, I'm at the end of my rope; all of the knots are being pulled and I've just nowhere to go now.' She then said, 'Excuse me.' She went into the apartment and got a handkerchief and came back out and wiped her eyes and sat back down and said, 'You see, that's one of the reasons I'm cleaning out all this junk now, so that when we move we won't have so much stuff to worry about.' I then asked Mrs Thompson where she was planning to move. She said, 'I don't know, find someplace I guess, I don't know.' I then asked her when were they going to move and Mrs Thompson said, 'When they throw us out of here, when they come and lock the door and set all our stuff outside, that's when we gon move cause we can't pay the rent and I don't see where any money is coming from so I just don't want to have all of this stuff setting out here when they lock us out of the house.'

Mrs Thompson was in constant trouble with the housing administration because of falling behind in her rent; they threatened to sue her and to throw her out, until they realized that she was a confused woman of exceedingly limited financial resources. Thus, at this point, David's problem is twofold: constant material insecurity and constant confusion, and an adult figure who, on the one hand, never knows where the money is going to come from to pay the rent, and, on the other, does not know how to protect the money she does have, by limiting expenditures.

Summarizing, one would have to say that the environment of David's home does not prepare him for the expectations of school. It would seem as if the stage were set for the conclusion that David's performance in school was miserable from the beginning and that 'he never had a chance', considering his background. Our studies of the two cases do not fit the stereotype.

Observations in David and Rachel's kindergarten class

Mrs B.: 'Michael, will you collect all the papers, please.' David said, 'Mrs B., can I help?' Mrs B.: 'He can do it by himself.'
Mrs B. left the room. . . . The noise level is 3. . . . David came up to me and asked, 'You want me to keep them quiet?' I told him that I was not in charge and he returned to his seat. . . . The noise level is up to 4. . . . David yells, 'Everybody be quiet! Be quiet!' The noise level drops to 3.

However, several months later he began to be inattentive in class, helping others with their work rather than doing his own, and getting into trouble with the teacher:

Everybody is at the weather dial paying attention except for David who is opposite me looking at a book. . . . Mrs B.: 'Who can tell us what the weather is outside today? Raise your hands. David.' David was running around the book table at this point. He didn't say anything. . . . Mrs B.: 'Let's come back to the piano, little people,' and everybody was over to the piano except David who is still running around the book table.

Mrs B.: 'Let's bow our heads,' and the class began saying the prayer. However, David, George, Frederick and Maurice were not paying attention.

To a considerable extent school for David is now an institution-alized version of the harsh, impersonal treatment he receives at home.

When I arrived in Mrs B's class, the children were seated around the piano and she was slapping some little boy (Benny) on the side of his head saying in time to the slaps, 'You will listen to me.' 11.30 Mrs B.: 'We will all wash our hands at one time, children. Do not wash your hands now, please.' 11.31. 'Children, what's wrong with your ears this morning? What did I just say?' She was referring to washing hands. 11.32. 'Billie,' and he says, 'Huh?' Mrs B.: 'Come here. . . . Where are you going?' Billie says, 'In the bathroom.' Mrs B.: 'For what?' Billie: 'To wash my hands.' Mrs B.: 'What did I just say? Boy, if you don't sit down,' and she paused, 'I'm going to spank you.'

Mrs B.: 'David, I asked you to use your hand, not your mouth.' She whipped David rather hard with the pointer.

Mrs B. returns and says, 'Little people, you are not to do anything with these papers. Now I didn't tell you that. All little people who have put something on your paper, ball the paper up and put it in the trash can, please.' About thirteen students do. . . . She reiterates about putting the paper in the can and says, 'You children are so hard-headed, why did you mark on that paper? I didn't say anything about it. You didn't know what I wanted to do with them.' Some little girl balls her paper and Mrs B hits her on the arm several times with the pointer and says, 'Why did you mark on this paper?' Then she says, 'Lock your lips. All those who have to throw papers away line up at the desk.' When they do so she gives them another piece of paper and says, 'You're going to have to get a spanking.' However, she does nothing to carry out her threat.

Mrs B.: 'Children, why did you draw lines? Why did you draw lines? I asked you not to make lines. You little people don't listen. Those of you who drew lines, put your papers in the waste can.

You'll have to do your papers over. You'll be behind the other children.'

Mrs B.: 'Little people, stand behind your chairs, don't bother with the crayon.' And the children still played with the crayon whereupon Mrs B. went over to David and hit him while she was saying in an angry voice, 'Keep your hands away from the crayon. You little people are hard-headed.' She really hit these kids this time.

Proper, correct behaviour is very rarely rewarded and about the only time Mrs B. appeared aware of the child as a person, as an individual, was in a punishment situation. Since Rachel was well-behaved, did as she was told and never volunteered, we have no observations on her that parallel those on David.

Results from kindergarten and first grade analysis

We give below a partial analysis of the data up to February 1966.

1. We coded observations of David and Rachel in kindergarten and first grade as follows:

(a) Shows leadership or helpfulness.
(b) Neglects work or acts up.
(c) Gives right answer to teacher's question.
(d) Gives wrong answer to teacher's question.
(e) Gives confused answer to teacher's question.

The results for the two children are as follows:

Table 1 Per cent of Type of Answers as related to Total Answers

	Kindergarten David	Rachel
Right answer	54	80
Wrong answer	20	19
Confused answer	26	1
Number of times showing leadership	8*	0
Number of times acting up	8*	0
	First grade	
Right answer	70	55
Wrong answer	30	45
Number of times inattentive	2*	0
Thumbsucking in class	2*	0

*The last two items are not percentages but acts.

2. In February 1966 the children received identical report cards in the first grade. The teacher's comment on the two children follows:

[The researcher reports] Mrs Trask told me that Rachel is a good student who usually thinks. She said the reason for Rachel's success in school appears to be more one of control and discipline than of capacity; with drive and push Rachel will be consistently good. David has it but he's not so controlled and he's getting into trouble in the school yard. He's becoming a behaviour problem. He's very aggressive and is generally a little tough boy and won't study his words.

David took to disappearing from home for many hours in the summer of 1965 and was beaten black and blue for it by his father, who was especially located for the purpose, but who definitely has no interest in David. David is beaten by James, who has created violent scenes in the household. David was recently whipped by the school principal for urinating on the playground. He was also seen by the researcher to be struck by the teacher in kindergarten. On the positive side: Mrs Trask, as contrasted with David's kindergarten teacher, is interested in him and plans so that he will perform at the best possible level in her class.

This brings us to the problem of the school.

The culture of the school

Whether or not David and Rachel will or will not succeed in school is a function of the interplay between the culture of the school and the culture outside. The question is: what do we mean by 'culture of the school'? The answer to the general question is obtained by getting answers to the following subsidiary questions among others:

1. What are the values, perceptions and attitudes of the people in the school? Since, when the child is in school, he is a member of the school culture, answers to the question apply to him just as well as to the school personnel. Thus for example, we study the class position of pupils, teachers, and principals; their values, their perceptions of one another, their attitudes towards the school, and so on. We want to know the *general* value orienta-

tions of school personnel as well as the values they use in judging one another and the pupils; and we want to know the same about the pupils. We want to know also how the pupils perceive the teachers and vice versa; how the teachers perceive one another and the principal and how he perceives them. We want to know what the attitudes of all the members of the school culture are toward the school itself.

2. What is the internal structure of the school? What is the hierachy of power in each school? Who are the pace setters, the cultural maximizers, the arbiters of value judgements? What are the roles of the teachers and the principal? How much freedom of choice is there for a teacher? What are the relative power positions of the newcomers and the old hands; the insiders and the outsiders (if any)? What in general are the lines of formal and informal communication and organization? Is it possible to evade the formal structure? Does it really exist? What is the relationship between types of structure and communication and getting anything done? What are the patterns of socialization of new teachers into the on-going 'tradition' of the particular school? What are the patterns of recruitment into the school? What are the 'quit' patterns? What processes determine turn-over, advancement, etc.?

3. What are the formal and informal relationships between the educational bureaucracy and 2?

4. What is the relationship between the parents and the school system?

5 What goes on in the classroom? The format of the answer to this question is given in 'A cross-cultural outline of education' (see Bibliography, p. 69).

The dynamic sum of the answers to questions 1 to 5 constitute the ethnography of the school; and from this one should be able to derive a general answer to the question: what is the culture of the (particular) school? This should yield an answer to a question like: why did David's kindergarten teacher hit him? At the end of the study, the answer to the question should look like this:* David's teacher hit him for the following rea-

* This is merely a paradigm, not a conclusion.

sons: 1. He acts up in a school which insists on strict order and discipline even in kindergarten (value of order). 2. The teacher is a middle-class teacher who devalues David because of his background. 3. The principal and teachers believe that the only thing that 'makes an impression on kids' is a strong arm. 4. The school district is under pressure to 'make a showing' and 'it's kids like David who give us all a black eye'. 5. The teacher's promotion is related to the achievement records of her children. 6. The principal is a 'no-nonsense' man who believes in holding a tight rein on his 'outfit'. 9. The principal knows he is under scrutiny by the district superintendent whose ambition it is to make a showing with his plan for bettering the condition of the children in his district. 10. Since David has his own emotional problems that do not allow him to toe the mark, he is often inattentive etc., and so arouses the teacher who, *under the conditions stated*, is prone to express her irritation with children by violence.

Model

If we let O stand for the outcome of David's total educational experience, E for his experience at home, P for his peer-group experience, and S for the influence of the school culture and T for time, then

$$O = f (E + S + P)T.$$

The fact that David's teacher struck him or that he succeeds in the first grade is a function of the influence of the school culture and of his relationships with his peers and of his life at home – in the widest sense, of an emotional as well as a cognitive experience. Complex as each of its elements is, the model suggests the following hypotheses, among others: 1. that the outcome of schooling depends on a complex of factors; 2. that if one factor, let us say E, takes on a largely negative significance – negative exceeds positive –this might be overcome if certain factors in S were maximized – like an improvement in teaching methods; 3. that if one factor is maximized – like, for an example, a great improvement in teaching methods – it might be cancelled by a negative indication in another, as in the home or peer group situation, for example. We have entered T as a *multiplier* with some hesitation, and with the reservation that *T is no more a simple multiplier than* $E+S+P$ *is a simple sum.* We have in mind the fact that the longer any process continues the greater effect it will have on the outcome. We add the time dimension also because the study is a life-historical one. Meanwhile, the presence of T suggests sampling O for particular children at particular times.

Conclusions and position

Understanding of the educational vicissitudes of children will be expanded by passing from correlational analysis of groups to the study of individual children in their natural habitat; and it is not only the culturally deprived that will be helped in this way but all children. Our findings, miniscule though they are at present, suggest the obvious: that the outcome of a child's experience with the formal educational system is the sum of several types of experience – home, school and peer group. Any one factor taken alone cannot explain why some fail and others succeed. Plans for improving the education of children must be based, therefore, on an understanding of the relationship among the factors. While we cannot know what is going on in the life of *every* child, we have to assume that among deprived children they always suffer a heavy burden of extra-curricular environmental disability. Provision ought to be made for it in the school culture. Most obvious is the training of teachers to handle these children. Too often, among Negro as well as among white teachers, the attitude toward the ghetto child is such as to make his life in school almost as harsh as his environment at home. The result is an accumulation of anxieties beyond the point where school learning is possible.

Bibliography

David P. Ausubel, 'A teaching strategy for culturally deprived pupils: cognitive and motivational considerations', *The School Review*, Winter 1963, pp. 454–63.

Basil Bernstein, 'Language and social class', *British Journal of Sociology*, vol. 11, 1960, pp. 271–5.

Basil Bernstein, 'Linguistic codes, hesitation phenomena and intelligence', *Language and Speech*, vol. 5, no. 1, 1962.

J. S. Bruner, *The Process of Education*, Harvard University Press, 1960.

J. S. Bruner, 'The cognitive consequences of early sensory deprivation', in Philip Solomon (ed.), *Sensory Deprivation*, Harvard University Press, 1961.

J. S .Bruner, 'The course of cognitive growth', *American Psychologist*, vol. 19, 1964, pp. 1–15.

Virginia Crandall, 'Achievement behavior in young children', *Young Children*, November 1964, pp. 77–90.

Martin Deutsch, 'Nursery education : the influence of social programming on early development', *Journal of Nursery Education*, April 1963, pp. 191–7.

Martin Deutsch, Papers from the Arden House Conference on Pre-school Enrichment in *Merrill–Palmer Quarterly of Behavior and Development*, vol. 10, 1964, pp. 207–8; 249–63.

Martin Deutsch, 'The role of social class in language development and cognition', *American Journal of Orthopsychiatry*, vol. 25, 1964, pp. 78–88.

Martin Deutsch, 'Some psychological aspects of language in the disadvantaged', paper presented at the Boston University Development Conference on the Teaching of Disadvantaged Youth, 1964.

Martin Deutsch, Alma Maliver, Bert Brown and Estelle Cherry, *Communication of Information in the Elementary School Classroom*, Cooperative Research Project no. 908, Institute for Developmental Studies, Department of Psychiatry, New York Medical College, 1964.

Jules Henry, 'Culture, education and communications theory', in George Spindler (ed.), *Education and Anthropology*, Stanford University Press, 1955.

Jules Henry, 'Culture, education and communications theory', in *Journal of Social Issues*, vol. 11, no. 2, 1955.

Jules Henry, 'Attitude organization in elementary school classrooms', *American Journal of Orthopsychiatry*, vol. 27, no. 1, 1957.

Jules Henry, 'The problem of spontaneity, initiative and creativity in suburban classrooms', *Journal of Orthopsychiatry*, vol. 29, no. 1, 1959.

Jules Henry, 'Cross-cultural outline of education', *Current Anthropology*, vol. 1, 1960, pp. 267–305.

Jules Henry, 'Golden rule days : American schoolrooms', in *Culture Against Man*, Random House, 1963.

Jules Henry, 'Death, fear and climax in nursery school play', in Peter Neubauer (ed.), *Concepts of Development in Early Childhood Education*, Charles C. Thomas, 1965.

Jules Henry, 'White people's time, colored people's time', *Trans-Action*, March/April, 1965.

Jules Henry, 'Hope, delusion and organization: some problems in the motivation of low achievers', in Lauren G. Woodby (ed.), *The Low Achiever in Mathematics*, US Department of Health, Education and Welfare, OE 29061, no. 31, 1965.

Jules Henry, *The Study of Families by Naturalistic Observation*, Psychiatric Research Report 30, American Psychiatric Association, 1966.

James L. Olson and Richard G. Larson, 'An experimental curriculum for culturally deprived kindergarten children', *Educational Leadership*, May 1965, pp. 553–8.

Vera P. John, 'The intellectual development of slum children', *American Journal of Orthopsychiatry*, vol. 33, 1963, pp. 813–22.

Frank Riessman, *The Culturally Deprived Child*, Harper & Row, 1962.

5 A Cross-Cultural Outline of Education*

Introduction

The names of many anthropologists have become associated with the cross-cultural study of education. Pettitt (1946), Raum (1940), Mead (1939) and Spiro (1958) have devoted entire volumes to the subject. A short but enlightening work is that of Fortes on the *Social and Psychological Aspects Of Education in Taleland* (1938). Volume 48 of the *American Journal of Sociology* (1943) contains several papers by anthropologists on education. A few anthropological monographs contain sections on education, though others make reference to the subject merely in passing. Recently, a review of problems in education appeared as a collaborative work of anthropologists and educators (Spindler, 1955).

In surveying these publications, it seemed that it might be useful if a general outline of the educational process could be provided for the anthropological field worker. With such an outline, the scientist would not need to rely solely on his creative imagination and on works that are often incomplete and focused on particularistic interests, for he would have available also a methodological tool that might help increase the scope of his observations.

As industrial cultures become more and more the target of anthropological interest, anthropologists will sooner or later have to study their educational systems too, so that an outline of education for anthropologists should take account not only of pre-literate culture but of industrial society also.

Much material that one might wish to see included in an outline of education is concerned largely with personality, with physiological pathways to enculturation, and with the conditioning of the very young child while feeding, eliminating, or, in general, in close physical contact with his family. The present outline, however, deals primarily, though not exclusively, with children about six years of age and older, and concentrates on the

*From *Current Anthropology*, vol. 1, no. 4, July 1960.

formal, conscious aspects of education. Furthermore, since the outline and text are concerned solely with education as a social process, no attention is given to knowledge the child acquires while alone.

Education can be looked at from the standpoint of the adult educator and from that of the child who is learning. The adult generally wants to do something to the child, and sees education as a process through which the child should become what the adult wants him to be. From the position of the child, however, education is also finding a way to certainty: the child wants to know what he should do about everything, and how he should do it, and he looks to the adult – to the educational process – to help him. This outline and text take account only of the first view.

Origins of the outline

While the outline derives in part from the work of others and in part from my own field experience in non-industrial cultures, much of it has grown out of research on cultural factors in learning that was begun seven years ago at Washington University. Several hundred protocols of direct observation of American classrooms have been collected by me and my students, and it was the analysis of these observations that made necessary the bulky (but by no means complete!) outline. The research continues (Henry, 1955a; 1955b; 1957a; 1957b; 1959).

The records collected during this research are factual, relatively unscreened process notes of what the observer saw. The major selective factor was the observer's concentration on teacher-pupil interaction.

Some theoretical problems

Humans must learn much more than other animals, and the evolution of *homo sapiens* has been characterized by a great expansion of his dependence on learning and of his capacity to learn. This has been accompanied by an increase in the number of teaching devices. For these reasons the outline contains a partial inventory of the materials humans must learn and of teaching methods.

Although in the past thirty years or so the dependence of

lower animals on learning has become apparent, due particularly to the work of the comparative psychologists, learning in *homo sapiens* differs from that in other animals in some striking ways. Among these are the following. 1. In man, learning is dominated by symbolic processes. 2. In man, the motivational organizers of learning are more variable – that is to say, much less subject to innate determinants than in sub-human species. 3. There are apparently, in man, no innate limits on learning : the outer limits of the capacity of human beings to learn have not yet been discovered. 4. A striking feature of man is the extent to which his learning is polyphasic (Henry, 1955a) that is, affected by a strong innate tendency to learn more than one thing at a time. While it is true, as Pavlov (1928) has shown, that animals also learn more than one thing at a time, polyphasic learning is much more extensive in man.

The combination in *homo sapiens* of genetic variability, absence of obvious, biologically determined limits on learning, and great capacity for polyphasic learning, has brought it about that the social processes of learning have become extremely complex, and therefore require long-sustained and meticulous observation and recording by the researcher. The net, but by no means final, result of an effort to catalogue the actual – as distinguished from laboratory – learning *events* in human children is a long and complicated outline like the one offered here. When, to this, we add the dimension of cultural variability, the catalogue becomes even more impressive. It then becomes clear that the education of humans cannot be understood through conceptually reducing the entire process to a simple regard-reinforcement system (Miller and Dollard, 1941).

The paradoxical aspect of human education is that in spite of the overshadowing tendency of human learning to variability and expansion, educational procedures have regularly taken as a model the innate release mechanism postulated by ethology (Tinbergen, 1951). That is to say, it would appear that human societies have tried repeatedly to accomplish in their members a completely predictable response system. The model, though not the reality, of the educated human, is the mass tendency of an American audience to rise to its feet whenever it hears the national anthem : the response is predictable and almost automatic. Teachers in

American elementary schools rely heavily on the culturally determined and learned tendency of children to raise their hands whenever the teacher wants the answer to a question; Pilagá mothers depend on the learned tendency of their children to recoil from the village boundaries or to duck into their houses whenever an adult shouts the term 'sorcerer'. The processes whereby these tendencies to respond predictably to single or complex symbols are internalized in the child form the matrix of education everywhere. This outline, particularly the sections on teaching methods (section II, pp. 80–82) and on conduct control section IX p. 87) attempts to take account of these processes.

Thus, as one peruses the outline, one cannot but be struck by the fact that what it represents, in part, is a measure of the extent to which human learning has departed from that of lower animals. Stated another way, if one wished to obtain an answer to the question, 'How does human learning differ from animals?' a first step might be to examine this outline, for here, quite apart from the general theoretical points raised, the mere catalogue of the dimensions of human education serves to place human learning on an entirely different plane from that of even the higher primates.

Further theoretical issues will be discussed in explaining the categories contained in the outline.

Explanation of the outline

The outline contains twelve major sections, each divided into many sub-sections. Only those sub-sections the titles of which do not seem self-explanatory will be discussed. I have tried to present here both an explanation of the outline and a theoretical orientation to problems of education in its cross-cultural aspects. I have attempted also to raise theoretical issues of anthropological relevance in so far as they relate to matters impinging on education. For this reason the chapter, in addition to being a set of explanatory notes, is also a collection of miniature theoretical essays.

A cross-cultural outline of education

I.   *On what does the educational process focus ?*
  1.   Environment (other than human)
      (a)   Flora
      (b)   Fauna
      (c)   Climate
      (d)   Geographical features
      (e)   Anthropomorphized flora
      (f)   Anthropomorphized fauna
      (g)   Anthropomorphized or zoomorphized machines
      (h)   Anthropomorphized or zoomorphized natural
            phenomena other than flora or fauna (winds, rivers,
            mountains, etc.)
      (i)   Space
      (j)   Time
      (k)   Motion
      (l)   Space-time-motion
      (m) The world view of the culture
        i.   Isolate-static
       ii.   Communicate-changing
              Engulfing
      iii.   Hostile or pacific
              Hostile
              Pacific
              Selectively hostile or pacific
       iv.   Geographical position of places studied
              Near: own town, state or province, village, tribe
              Near-distant: other states or provinces, nation in
              general; other villages or tribes
              Distant: other lands
        v.   Temporal position
              Immediate
              Contemporary
              Near past
              Distant past
              Mythological past
      (n)   Clothing
      (o)   Food
      (p)   Transportation and communication

2. Values
   (a) Good and bad: moral rules
   (b) Work, success, failure
   (c) Being on time
   (d) Culture
   (e) Proper dress
   (f) Strength, activity, power
   (g) Beating the game
   (h) Politeness, tact
   (i) Cooperation, helpfulness, togetherness
   (j) Patriotism
   (k) Cleanliness, orderliness
   (l) Thrift, saving, don't waste
   (m) Parents are good
   (n) Prettiness, beauty
   (o) Love
   (p) Mother, motherhood
   (q) Happiness
   (r) Competitiveness
   (s) Equality
   (t) Novelty, excitement
   (u) Pride
   (v) Knowledge as value
   (w) The 'beautiful person'
   (x) Private property
   (y) Democracy
   (z) Family
   (a^1) Responsibility
   (b^1) Generosity, doing more than required, non-commercialism
   (c^1) The state
   (d^1) Defence
   (e^1) Enlightened self-interest
   (f^1) Independence, toughness
   (g^1) Physical intactness
   (h^1) Sense of emergency
   (i^1) Constancy
   (j^1) Solicitude for others, kindness
   (k^1) Composure under stress
   (l^1) Courage

(m^1) Knowledge as means to an end
(n^1) Compromise
(o^1) Fun, relaxation
(p^1) Friends, friendship, faithfulness
(q^1) Fairness
(r^1) Flattery, empty praise
(s^1) Honour (integrity), personal autonomy
(t^1) Self-restraint
(u^1) Trying hard, don't give up
(v^1) Fame, ambition
(w^1) Honesty
(x^1) Prestige
(y^1) Niceness, likeableness
(z^1) Respect for authority
(a^2) Excitement
(b^2) Gentleness, non-violence
(c^2) Speed, alertness
(d^2) Sacredness, etc., of parents
(e^2) Flexibility
(f^2) Modesty
(g^2) Tolerance
(h^2) Freedom
(i^2) Peace
(j^2) Progress
(k^2) Wealth
(l^2) USA
(m^2) Loyalty
(n^2) Money, greed, etc. are corrupting
(o^2) Smartness, cleverness, thinking
(p^2) Profit
(q^2) Size

2a. Value conflict
3.   Institutions
     (a)   Social structure
     (b)   Religion
     (c)   Economic system
4.   Technology, machines
5.   Reading, writing and arithmetic

6. Social manipulation
   (a) Recognition-seeking behaviour
   (b) Manipulation of others
   (c) Manipulation of self
7. Responsibility
8. How to compete
9. How to take care of others
10. Use of the mind
   (a) How to think
   (b) Disjunction
      i. When to disjoin
      ii. How to disjoin
      iii. From what to disjoin
   (c) Concentration
      i. Interest stimulation defining purpose; motivation
      ii. Force
      iii. Shutting out external stimuli
      iv. Visualization
      v. Focused retention
   (d) Preparation of the mind
   (e) 'Mental discipline'
11. Body parts or functions
   (a) The voice
   (b) The sphincters
   (c) Care of the body (like getting enough rest)
   (d) Posture
   (e) How to relax
   (f) The mouth
12. Art
13. History
14. Some other facts about which information is communicated
   (a) About systems of rewards and punishments
   (b) About what the culture promises its members
   (c) About permitted and forbidden activities
   (d) About how to get pleasure and avoid pain
   (e) About whom to love and whom to hate
   (f) How to handle frustration

> (g) The difference between the real and the manifest
>   (this refers to situations in which an effort is
>   deliberately made to enable the child to see
>   'behind' the obvious)
> (h) About death
> (i) About sex relations
> (j) About race, class, or ethnic differences

15. Instruction in identifiable adult tasks
    (a) Teaching about adult tasks
16. Scientific abstractions
17. Science (general)
18. Routine procedures
19. Childish handiwork
20. Cultural stereotypes
21. Warfare and associated activities
22. Safety
23. Songs, music
24. Mythology
25. The object system
26. Games
27. Cultural fictions

II. *How is the information communicated (teaching methods)?*
1. By imitation
2. By setting an example
3. By instruction in schools, ceremonials, or other formal
   institutions
4. By use of punishments
5. By use of rewards
6. Problem-solving
7. Guided recall
8. Giving the child tasks to perform beyond his immediate
   capacity
    (a) Jamming the machine
9. Mechanical devices
10. By kinaesthetic association
11. By experiment
    (a) By teacher
    (b) By pupil
12. By doing
13. By symbolic association

14. By dramatization
15. By games or other play
16. By threats
    (a) By trials
17. By irrelevant association
18. By relevant association
19. Through art
    (a) Graphic
    (b) Music, general
    (c) Songs
    (d) Literature (stories, myths, tales, etc.)
20. By stating the opposite of the truth
    ('Water's a solid, isn't it?'); writing antonyms
21. By holding up adult ideals
22. Acting in undifferentiated unison
23. Physical force
24. By positive or negative assertion
25. Repetition
26. By specifically relating information to the child's own
    body, bodily function or experience
27. Through ego-inflation
    (a) Through ego-deflation
28. Through use of humour
29. By telling
30. By watching
31. By listening
32. Question and answer
    (a) Teacher question, pupil answer
    (b) Pupil question, teacher answer
33. Holding up class, ethnic, national, or religious ideals
34. By doing something on his own
35. By repeating the child's error to him
    (a) By repeating the child's correct answer
36. By accusing
37. By following a model
    (a) Human
    (b) Non-human
38. By comparison
39. By filling in a missing part

40. By associative naming (e.g. a book mentions gingham as a material, and teacher asks students if they can name other materials)
41. By identifying an object (like going to the board and underlining a 'noun' in a sentence)
42. By group discussion
    (a) By class discussion
43. Physical manipulation
    (a) Bodily manipulation
    (b) Bodily mutilation and other physical stresses
44. Rote memory
45. By working together with a student (as when teacher and student work together to make a battery, or as when teacher and student go over reference books together)
46. Through special exhibits
47. By having children read substantive materials (e.g. reading the chemistry lesson in the reader)
48. By putting the child on his mettle ('Now let's see how well you can read.')
49. Through group projects
50. By giving procedural instructions
51. By demanding proof
52. Through reports by students
53. By pairing (e.g., one child gives a word and calls on another child to give a sentence with the word; one child gives the state and another gives the capital)
54. By asking for volunteers
55. Through isolating the subject

III. *Who educates?*
  1. Males or females?
  2. Relatives or others?
  3. On which age group doe the burden of education fall?
     (a) Peers
       i. Boy
       ii. Girl
     (b) Older children
       i. Male
       ii. Female

    (c)   Adolescents
    i.   Male
    ii.   Female
    (d)   Adults
    i.   Male or female
    ii.   Younger or older
    iii.   Married or unmarried
    (e)   Others

4. Is education by 'successful' people?
5. What rewards accrue to the educator?
    (a)   Enhanced status
    (b)   Material rewards
    (c)   Emotional satisfactions
6. Are there education specialists?
7. Does the educator wear distinctive dress or other insignia?
8. Is the educator of the same or of a different social group from that of the person being educated? (national, racial, class, etc.)

IV. *How does the person being educated participate?*
    (what is his attitude?)
1. Accepting
2. Rejecting, resistive
3. Bored, indifferent
4. Defiant
5. Inattentive
6. Social closeness of teacher and child
7. Social distance of teacher and child
8. Finds the process painful?
9. Finds the process gratifying?
10. Competitively
    (a)   Cooperatively
11. With inappropriate laughter
    (a)   Ridiculing peers
12. Laughter at humour of peers or teacher
13. Overt docility
14. Eagerly
    (a)   Facial expression
    (b)   Hand-raising
    (c)   Talking out

      (d) Heightened bodily tonus

15. Through making independent decisions and suggestions
16. Asks for clarification, direction, etc.
17. Through spontaneous contributions or other demonstrations not precisely within the context of the lesson
18. Through spontaneous contributions within the context of the lesson
19. Attentively
20. Spontaneously humorous
21. Spontaneously expressive
22. Approaches teacher physically
23. Mobile—free
24. Immobile—constricted
25. Through performing special assigned tasks
26. Hostile to peers
      (a) Protective of peers
27. Diversion to peers
28. Anxiously
29. Disjoined hand-raising
30. By whispering to teacher
31. Laughs at peers
32. Corrects teacher
33. Disruptively
      (a) Critically
34. By carping criticism
35. By praising work of peers
36. Dishonesty, cheating, lying, etc.
37. Attempts to maintain order
38. Guiltily
39. With sense of inadequacy
40. With sense of adequacy
41. By copying from peers
42. Attempts to control the class
43. No response
44. Uses teacher's last name
45. Uses teacher's first name
46. Calls out to teacher
47. Uses kinship term
48. By public performance

V.   *How does the educator participate ? (what is his attitude ?)*
1.   Eagerly
    (a)   Facial expression
    (b)   Bodily movement
    (c)   Tone of voice
    (d)   Heightened bodily tonus
2.   Bored, uninterested, etc.
3.   Embarrassed
4.   Dominative
    (a)   Integrative
5.   Insecure
6.   Politely
7.   Enjoys correct response
8.   Resents incorrect response
9.   Can't tell
10.   Seeks physical contact with person being educated
11.   Acceptance of blame
12.   Putting decisions up to the children
13.   Discouraging
14.   Encouraging
15.   Hostile, ridiculing, sarcastic, belittling
16.   Relatively mobile
17.   Relatively immobile
18.   Personalizing
    (a)   Use of request sentence with name
    (b)   Use of name only
    (c)   Use of hand-name technique
    (d)   Use of equalizing, levelling term like 'comrade'
19.   Depersonalizing
    (a)   Use of class seating plan for recitation in succession
    (b)   Use of 'next' or some such impersonal device
    (c)   Use of 'you' instead of name
    (d)   Pointing nodding, looking.
20.   Irritable
21.   Accepts approach
22.   Repels approach
23.   Accepting of child's spontaneous expressions
24.   Rejecting of child's spontaneous expressions
25.   Humorous
26.   Handles anxiety, hostility, discomfort, etc.

27. Acts and/or talks as if child's self-image is fragile
28. Acts and/or talks as if child's self-image is irrelevant
29. Defends child against peers
30. Responds to non-verbal cue other than hand-raising
31. Excessively polite
32. Keeps word
33. Fails to keep word
34. Praises and rewards realistically
35. Praises and rewards indiscriminately
36. Critical (does not point out good things in student's work)
37. Does not reward correct answer or good performance
38. Does not punish incorrect answer or poor performance
39. Acknowledges own error
40. Uses affectional terms like 'honey' or 'dear'
41. Awakens anticipation
('Now we are going to get some nice new books.')
42. The inclusive plural

VI. *Are some things taught to some and not to others?*
1. Do different age groups learn different things?
2. Do the sexes learn different things?
3. Are different groups taught different things?

VII. *Discontinuities in the educational process*
1. Discontinuities between age-periods
(a) In regard to techniques
(b) In regard to values
2. How do all of these apply between the sexes?
(a) Are discontinuities different for boys and girls?
(b) The secrecy of initiation rites

VIII. *What limits the quantity and quality of information a child receives from a teacher?*
1. Methods of teaching
2. Available time
3. Quality of equipment
4. Distance from the object
5. Ignorance or error of teacher
6. Stereotype of the object
7. Failure of teacher to correct pupil's mistakes

8. Failure of teacher to indicate whether the pupil's answers are right or wrong
9. Failure of teacher to respond to a question
10. General vagueness or fumbling of the teacher

IX. *What forms of conduct control (discipline) are used?*
1. Relaxed
2. Tight
3. Sense of propriety
4. Affectivity
5. Reprimand
   (a) Direct
   (b) Gentle
   (c) Mixed ('We like for you to have an opinion but it is childish for you to shout out your numbers like that.')
   (d) Impersonal ('Some of you are holding us up.')
6. Ridicule
7. Exhortation ('How can I teach you if you keep making so much noise?')
8. Command
9. Command question or request
10. 'We' technique
11. Instilling guilt
12. Cessation of activity
13. Group sanction
14. Threat
15. Putting the child on his mettle
16. Non-verbal signal
17. Reward
18. Promise of reward
19. Special stratagems
20. Awakening fear
21. Using a higher power
    (a) Human
    (b) Non-human
22. Exclusion
23. Punishment
24. Encourages peer-group control

X.   *What is the relation between the intent and the results of education ?*
1.   Relatively high correlation between intention and results
2.   Relatively low correlation between intention and results

XI.   *What self-conceptions seem reinforced ?*
1.   Ego-forming factors
   (a)   Syntonic: praise, support, status inflation —
         Grandiose self-conception
   (b)   Dystonic: blame, shame, guilt, fright, exclusion —
         Depersonalization

XII.   *How long does the process of formal education last ?*

I. ON WHAT DOES THE EDUCATIONAL PROCESS FOCUS?
The first step in a discussion of the educational process must be
to make a reasonably complete catalogue of what is taught. The
outline is an attempt to do this, from the point of view of what
an observer can rather readily see with the naked eye. The theoretical point in this section is that, in humans, behaviour is everywhere organized relative to a specific universe that is culturally
determined, and that, accordingly, we need to know for each such
universe what subject matter education includes. On the other
hand, since, in each culture, an effort is made to exclude perceptions not relevant to its universe, education is also a process of
exclusion (see I. 10. (b)).

I: 1. *Environment (other than human)*
In this section are catalogued factors in the natural, non-human
environment, in the broadest sense, and no attention is given to
their 'inner meaning'. However, it does appear relevant to point
out that, whereas a primitive child's knowledge of the flora and
fauna in his environment generally has direct survival-relevance,
this natural world of flora, fauna, and even weather is largely
peripheral to the life of the child in industrial cultures.

I: 1: (e). Anthropomorphized flora; I: 1: (f). Anthropomorphized fauna; I: 1: (g). Anthropomorphized or zoomorphized
machines; I: 1: (h). Anthropomorphized or zoomorphized
natural phenomena other than flora or fauna (winds, rivers,
mountains, etc.)

One of the principal functions of anthropomorphized animals is to serve as a medium for the transmission of values. The *Panchatantra* of India is an excellent example of this from a literate culture. In the life of young children in industrial cultures, this function overshadows the real aspects of animals. Everywhere, flora and other non-animal natural phenomena function less in this way.

The use of anthropomorphized and zoomorphized machines as vehicles for general ideas is well illustrated in Ilin's *The Story of the Great Plan*. Written to acquaint Soviet boys and girls twelve to fourteen years old with the Five Year Plan launched in 1928, it appeared in English under the title *New Russia's Primer* (1931). Ilin makes vivid and poetic use of anthropomorphized and zoomorphized machines and natural phenomena to communicate to children a breathless, value-laden excitement about the Great Plan. Some examples will illustrate the point.

There is a giant excavator. It has only one arm, but this arm is twenty metres in length. In its hand it holds a shovel. . . . The scoop cuts into the ground with teeth made of forged steel and is filled with earth. . . . The giant excavator turns to the left in a circle, as a soldier at a drill (pp. 30–31).

Wind, water, coal, wood, may not be alive, but they can be forced to work. They can be compelled to turn the wheels of machines. In Baku the wind flaps the wings of a windmill . . . (p. 33).

Our mountains and plains are well supplied with rivers. These rivers could give us sixty-five million horsepower of electrical energy. But to compel them to work for us is not so easy. Man must fight the river, as the animal-tamer tames wild beasts. If he becomes careless only for a moment, he will make a mistake and the beast will spring upon him and tear him to pieces (pp. 35–6)

It would appear that the function of this kind of writing is to bring the children closer to the machines and the land in order to adapt the children to the requirements of the economic effort.

I : 1 : (l). Space-time-motion
An example of teaching materials involving simultaneous consideration of space, time, and motion is the statement that, 'It

takes a plane travelling X miles an hour, Y hours to get from B to C.'

I : 1 : (m) The world view of the culture

I : 1 : (m) : i. *Isolate-static.* A culture with an 'isolate-static' world view sees itself as isolated from the rest of the world, fixed in respect to its spatial orientation on the earth's surface, and static in regard to change. This is typical of the *Gemeinshaft* type of society.

I : 1 : (m) : ii. *Communicate-changing.* A culture with a 'communicate-changing' world view is in communication with the surrounding world, is expansive in regard to its orientation on the earth's surface, and dynamic in regard to change. This is a world outlook in which the members of the society see themselves in contaces with the rest of the world and are oriented toward change. The attitude is characteristic of the *Gesellschaft.*

I : 1 : (m) : ii. *Communicate-changing (Engulfing).* The culture with an 'engulfing' world view is one that views itself as conquering and swallowing up other cultures. This would characterize the Nazi world view (Childs, 1938, pp. 107 *et seq.*) and the Inca world view.

I : 1 : (m) : iii. *Hostile or pacific (Selectively hostile or pacific).* Some groups divide the world into friend and foe, and attempt to instil in children hostility toward foes and acceptance toward friends. The Kaingáng, however (Henry, 1941), have no friends outside the narrow group of the extended family, and view themselves as surrounded by enemies. Something similar seems to characterize the Sirionó (Holmberg, 1950), but particularly with respect to the band.

I : 1 : (m) : v. *Temporal position (Mythological past).* Subject matter from the mythological past is a category delineated from the point of view of the ethnographer, since, as some peoples see it, there is no separation between the real and the mythological past. For example, there are many people nowadays to whom the biblical story of Jonah who, swallowed by a whale, lived inside it, may still be true. The distinction made by the ethnographer is one of convenience, and he can always explain the native attitude.

I : 2. *Values*

In the course of the research, no less than sixty-nine values were tabulated. This is partly because 'value' was construed to mean any normative idea or sentiment, in Radcliffe-Brown's sense, that serves as an organizer of culturally standardized behaviour. Thus honesty (I : 2 : w[1]) has been listed as a value, but so have dishonesty, deception, and chicanery (I : 2 : g) because they too are normative organizers, as among the Alor and Chagga (Du Bois, 1944, pp. 64, 65, 66; Raum, 1940, pp. 210, 211). Values are dealt with here without reference to what is expressed in the ongoing life of the culture.

A focus on values in the study of educational processes has implications not only for understanding the organization of behaviour, but also for understanding polyphasic learning, since education, the fundamental organizing process, occurs always in a context of values, and teachers are usually teaching values by implication, regardless of the immediate subject matter. When, for example, a Pilagá mother tells her baby to give his food to a relative (Henry and Boggs, 1952), the baby's behaviour is being organized with respect to a particular group of people at the same time that he is learning it is good to give food away. In the example quoted above from *New Russia's Primer*, the values of challenge, mastery, bigness, man-over-nature (Kluckhohn, 1951), compulsion, struggle, danger, vigilance and mechanization all appear in a text acquainting the children with the Five Year Plan and what must be done to effect it.

Values may be openly asserted, such as, 'It is good to work hard'; be expressed indirectly, as in the *Primer* (Ilin, 1931); or be conveyed in a situation, such as in the East European Jewish *shtetl* where children had to work hard at their studies all day long in the *kheder*, early elementary school (Zborowski and Herzog, 1952, p. 89), with no appeal to 'fun-in-learning'. Of Ilin's book, one may say that it 'breathes an ideology'. Soviet education (Counts and Lodge, 1947) is very sensitive to values, and, to judge from Counts's and Lodge's book, faces squarely any problems connected with them. This is true also of *kibbutz* education in Israel (Spiro, 1958, p. 256). Meanwhile, there is always the question of the relation between ideology and results, and this ought to be studied in all educational systems. In this connection, one difficulty is that a teacher's own unconscious behaviour may contradict the values he is attempting to teach; another is that the educational system may attempt to emphasize contradictory values (see I : 2a).

I : 2 : (w) The 'beautiful person'

The 'beautiful person' refers to an ideal best described in the literature for traditional China and the Jewish *shtetl*. The following from Zborowski and Herzog (1952, p. 81) expresses the idea. Speaking of the *talmid khokhem*, the 'wise student and scholar', they say :

He is not even expected to know the value of money, but it is taken for granted that the keenness of his mind, sharpened by lifelong study, will allow him to penetrate the most complicated business.

A talmid khokhem, a wise scholar, is easily recognizable in the streets of the shtetl. He walks slowly, sedately, absorbed in his thoughts. His speech is calm, rich in quotations from the Bible or the Talmud, allusive and laconic – his words 'are counted like pearls'. He is greeted first by other members of the community, in deference to his high position. Not only the poor but also the wealthy greet him first, if they are less learned than he. . . .

A learned man seldom laughs aloud. Excessive laughter, like any sort of excess, is considered the mark of an amorets [boor]. . . . The talmid khokhem must indicate his dignity and sophistication by his behaviour and his appearance.

The shtetl ideal of male beauty again reflects the high value set on learning. A man with *hadras ponim*, a distinguished, beautiful face, ideally has a long beard – symbol of age and therefore of wisdom. His forehead is high, indicating well-developed mentality; his complexion is pale, revealing long hours spent over books. Thick eyebrows showing penetration jut out over deep-set, semi-closed eyes, indicating weariness from constant poring over texts – eyes that shine and sparkle as soon as an intellectual problem is discussed. Very important are the pale, delicate hands, evidence that the owner has devoted his life to exercise of the mind rather than of the body.

The relevance of such a value to this study is that it anchors moral and behavioural ideology to a fixed image, which serves as a guide to the organization of general cultural behaviour. For students of social organization and disorganization – for the understanding of problems of anomie – it is important to examine the difference in functioning between societies that have such guides and those that do not. A problem of contemporary society is that it has no beautiful people – only beautiful actresses.

I : 6. Social manipulation

The teaching of social manipulation looms large in all cultures but is given relatively little attention in anthropological monographs or in writings on education. 'Social manipulation' includes all techniques for getting along with other people and for using people as instruments for survival, social mobility, and so on. Training in 'being nice to people', in smiling, in ingratiation, etc. fall under this I : 6. Outstanding among techniques of recognition-seeking (I : 6 : (a)) in American schools is, of course, the raised hand. 'Manipulation of self' (I : 6 : (c)) refers to training in how to handle one's self: role-taking, and self-restraint in social situations, fall in this category.

I : 10. Use of the mind

I : 10 : (a). How to think

Nowadays, in America, there is much talk about teaching children to think. In five years of observation in American schools, however, we have found very little behaviour that tends in this direction, and, therefore, this category is not expanded in the outline (in contrast, for example, to I : 10 : (c)). Thinking would seem to involve an analytical process of some kind and also a process of synthesis. Almost none of this takes place in elementary school (though we have found it occasionally), and little more even in high-school science courses.* Our research has not discovered in primitive societies emphasis on teaching children to think.

I : 10 : (b). Disjunction

The category 'Disjunction' refers to situations in which the child becomes a non-participant, or in which the environment behaves in one way and the child *withdraws* instead of behaving in the expected manner. The American child who keeps his hand raised in the air regardless of what is taking place in the classroom is

* In the United States the first eight years of school are called elementary-school, grammar school, or the primary grades. They are for children from six to fourteen years of age. The next four years are called high or secondary school. After completion of high school the individual is ready for college.

typical. In general, this category refers to all those situations in which the child withdraws mentally from the environment. This is the 'It-does-not-concern-me' effect, or the 'I-dismiss-it-from-my-mind' effect.

Training in disjunction occurs at every level in American schools, and most of it occurs without conscious effort by the adult. Rather, the adult, notably the classroom teacher, is constantly concerned to prevent disjunction. Nevertheless, lessons in subjects in which children are not interested, for example, are lessons in disjunction, for the children become detached from the subject matter, and, in an effort to escape from boredom may cast about – through daydreaming, drawing, or reading a forbidden book under the desk – for some way of escaping from the situation. Since the child discovers that one or another of these techniques is psychologically rewarding, he tends to revert to it whenever the uninteresting subject matter comes up, and, in this way, becomes educated in disjunction. The child who keeps his hand up in class even though he does not know what is going on – as evidenced by his confusion if the teacher calls on him – is one who disjoins from the subject matter but remains in touch with the social requirements of the situation. The capacity to dismiss things from one's mind – to 'filter out' unwanted stimuli – is an important capacity in a complex culture like that of the United States where one is always in danger of being inundated by stimuli. The process of disjunction, in the sense intended here, is not described in the literature for non-industrial civilizations, though it did occur in traditional China (Yang, 1945, pp. 145, 147; Williams, 1849, p. 434) and in the East European Jewish *shtetl* schools (Zborowski and Herzog, 1952, pp. 88, 104).

Dismissing a thing from the mind is one of the general process of filtering. At the beginning of section I (see p. 88), it was remarked that all cultures organize behaviour with respect to their own culturally selected portion of the universe. This must mean that education attempts to exclude from perception (filter out) all aspects of the surroundings not included in the culturally delimited universe. We know, in a systematic way, practically nothing about how adults train children to exclude from perception everything that does not belong in the culturally-standardized perceptual universe.

The narrowing of the perceptual field is accomplished in part through emphasizing only certain things during education. By this process, nothing that is not emphasized will be learned by the child. Meanwhile, since humans are inveterate polyphasic learners (Henry, 1955a), the process is never completely effective, and the resultant educational failure must be one of the sources of sociocultural conflict and change. We may speculate that very stable cultures have perfected, or nearly perfected, the process of narrowing the child's perceptual field – of training the child to dismiss from his mind anything not selected for his perceptions by the culture.

In section II, we will consider in more detail this process of narrowing the perceptual field.

I : 10.(c). Concentration
I : 10 : (c) : ii. *Force.* The use of force to compel students to concentrate is described by Zborowski and Herzog (1952, pp. 89–104) for the East European Jewish *shtetl* culture where children in the *kheder*, the earliest years of school, were struck by the teacher if their attention wandered.

I : 10 : (c) : v. *Focused retention.* 'Focused retention' refers to efforts to achieve concentration on the part of the child by obliging him to focus on textual materials. Thus, in reading in elementary schools, the children, through being required to answer questions about stories, learn to fix their minds on the details of the text.

I : 16 : *Scientific abstractions*; I : 17. *Science (general)*
The difference between 'scientific abstractions' and 'science (general)' may be exemplified as follows. In the former, instruction is given in the nature of electricity, while in the latter, the child is taught how to make a battery. In the former, a student in biology is taught that the cell is the basic building block of all organisms, while in the latter, he is told the structure of the cell.

I : 18. *Routine procedures*
'Routine procedures' has to do with actions such as distributing books, collecting papers on which the children have done their lessons, and so on.

I : 19. *Childish handiwork*
Making valentines, mat-like holders for pots, etc. – all those

time-killing activities that help fill the day in many American elementary schools – fall into the category of 'childish handiwork'. On the other hand, one ought not to include here the making of seed necklaces, flower chains, etc. that are *used* by the children in their games (Gorer, 1938, pp. 308–9; Chandhuri, 1951, p. 21). Rather, where such activity is taught by adults, one ought to delineate a separate, appropriate category, such as 'how to make toys or game-relevant objects'.

I : 25. *The object system*
In all societies material culture is part of a complex of inter-personal relations, values, beliefs and patterns of spatial arrangements. For example, in American culture a stove is made, owned, sold and bought as private property. As part of the American system of values, however, it not only expresses the value of private ownership, but, by its quality and form, expresses a standard of living, which is also held as a value. Furthermore, children and adult males are generally aloof from stoves, and although this is changing, it is on the whole still true that in American homes most of the time it is women who operate the stove. Again, stoves are sold not only in terms of their beauty and cost, but also in terms of their capacity to heat rapidly, which thereby gives expression to the value of speed. Finally, in regard to patterns of spatial arrangement, stoves are almost always kept in the kitchen, sometimes in the living room – if the living room is in a modern, compact apartment, where the kitchen may be separated from the living room merely by a difference in furnishings, including the stove – and never in a bedroom. The complex of associations that attaches to objects of material culture is here called the 'object system', and it is one of the principal foci of education in all societies. Mead says of Manus children (1939, pp. 32–3):

In Manus where property is sacred and one wails for lost property as for the dead, respect for property is taught children from their earliest years. Before they can walk they are rebuked and chastised for touching anything which does not belong to them. . . . The slightest breakage is punished without mercy. Once a canoe from another village was anchored near one of the small islands. Three little eight-year-old girls climbed on the deserted canoe and knocked a pot into the sea, where it struck a stone and broke. All night the village rang with drum calls and angry speeches, accusing, deprecating, apologizing for the damage done and denouncing careless children. The fathers made speeches of angry shame and described how roundly they had beaten the young criminals. The children's companions, far from admiring a daring crime, drew away from them in haughty disapproval and mocked them in chorus.

It can be seen from these examples that the object system is the broader system within which an economic system $(I:3:(c))$ may fit. 'Economic system' refers to patterns of production, distribution, and consumption of objects, while 'object system' refers to objects in all their aspects. When a child in an American elementary school is taught to collect books and *put them in the closet,* the knowledge that books belong in a closet is knowledge about the object system, while the relevance of that knowledge to the economic system is rather remote.

I : 27. *Cultural fictions*

A 'cultural fiction' is an idea known by at least one group in the culture to be untrue. There comes a time in the life of a person in such a culture when he learns that the idea is a fiction. For example, the Chagga fiction that men do not defecate is revealed as untrue to Chagga boys at initiation (Raum, 1940 p. 248); and the Hopi fiction that the dancing figures in the plaza are gods is revealed as a fiction also at initiation (Eggan, 1956). Thus learning a cultural fiction refers to the revelation of the fictional nature of an idea.

It is not always clear what the function of the revelation itself is. In Hopi (Eggan, 1956), the revelation seems to precipitate a reorganization of the personality in the effort to manage the overwhelmingly shocking realization of the deception that has been worked on one, and to accelerate 1. a turning away from childish ways, 2. a turning toward adulthood, and 3. a turning inward of the personality toward self-examination and self-criticism. While 1 and 2 seem to be present in Chagga also, there is no evidence of 3. Rather, there appears the development of an extreme insecurity of men with respect to women, and a concomitant hostility. On the other hand, it may be, also, that the men's awareness that psychologically they are frauds may be an added incentive to them to attempt to validate themselves as genuine warriors and workers.

Hopi and Chagga practice represent formalizations of the widespread use of fictions for the achievement of various cultural goals. Actually, fictions seem to have dysfunctional effects in the long run: even the Hopi case, so sympathetically described by Eggan, seems to have had long-run disfunctional effects in residual hostility and oppressive guilt.

II. HOW IS THE INFORMATION COMMUNICATED (TEACHING METHODS)?

Pettitt (1946; pp. 40 *et seq.*) has emphasized the importance of knowing exactly what techniques adults use to teach children. This section is devoted to the elucidation of the problem of specificity in reporting such data. The following quotations illustrate certain excellences and certain shortcomings:

> Eskimo mothers begin exercising the arms of young infants in the motions of paddling . . . (Pettitt, 1946, p. 43).

> Freuchen illustrates the eagerness of Eskimo parents to encourage hunting pursuits by young children. A three year old boy, Megusak, happened to sight a distant polar bear before anyone else saw it. He was praised mightily, and when the bear was killed a spear was put into his hands so that he could give it a poke, whereupon they praised him more (Pettitt, 1946, p. 43).

> When [a Manus boy] is about a year old, he has learned to grasp his mother firmly about the throat, so that he can ride in safety, poised on the back of her neck. She has carried him up and down the long house, dodged under low-hanging shelves, and climbed up and down the rickety ladders which lead from house floor down to the landing verandah. The decisive angry gesture with which he was reseated on his mother's neck whenever his grip tended to slacken has taught him to be alert and sure-handed (Mead, 1939, p. 23).

The description of the Eskimo mother exercising her infant in the motions of paddling could hardly be more specific, except to state more precisely how the baby's hands were held and, perhaps, whether the mother sang a song, and so on. The second example is strikingly specific. What is lacking is some statement to the effect that the child was *told* to poke the bear. The example from Manus would be better if we were told how the child learned to grasp its mother about the throat. On the other hand, the observation that the mother reseats the baby on her neck with a 'decisive angry gesture' is the kind of specificity needed to clarify the learning process.

In contrast, the following is vague :

By the time a boy is three years of age he is already pulling on some kind of bow, and with his companions he spends many hours shooting his weapons at any non-human target that strikes his fancy ... and when his marksmanship is perfected he is encouraged to stalk woodpeckers and other birds that light on branches near the house.

... the boy gradually learns when, where and how to track and stalk game. His father allows him to take easy shots, so as to reinforce his interest in hunting. ... During all this time, of course, he is also learning to make bows and arrows ... (Holmberg, 1950, p. 378).

The reason the description is vague is because we are not told how the boy is taught to pull 'on some kind of bow', how his marksmanship comes to improve, how the boy is 'encouraged to stalk woodpeckers', or how he learns to track game or make bows and arrows.

The purpose of section II is to raise in all its complexity the question of the specificity of teaching methods.

II : 1. *By imitation*
In his chapter on 'Imitation versus stimulated learning', Pettitt attack the uncritical use of the term 'imitation', pointing out that most of what has been called imitation is really 'directed practice' (Pettitt, 1946, p. 44) under the stimulation and guidance of adults. He reserves the term 'imitation' for learning experiences in which the child *spontaneously* copies a human model. Pettitt also provides a host of examples of child learning that are accounted for under separate headings in the outline. Molecular analysis of the educational process makes the category 'imitation' a residual one in which may be placed all examples of copying that do not fall into *other* categories in this section, most specifically :

II :   2. *By setting an example*
       12. *By doing*

15. *By games or other play*
30. *By telling*
31. *By watching*
32. *By listening*
37. *By following a model*
    (a) Human
    (b) Non-human

II : 3. *By instruction in schools, ceremonials,*
        or other formal institutions
The ceremonial initiation is a common device for educating children in primitive cultures. The Murngin (Warner, 1937) and Chagga (Raum, 1940) are good examples. Schools, that is, relatively permanent buildings especially dedicated to education, are not familiar outside of the literate civilizations. In undeveloped forms of education in the literate cultures, teachers' homes have been used (Zborowski and Herzog, 1952, p. 89; Bayne-Powell, 1939, pp. 57, 61). Poor Arabs in Egypt have built simple schools (*maktab*) for instruction in the Koran (Ammar, 1954, p. 206). The use of buildings for systematic instruction, whether a teacher's home or a separate school building, seems to be associated with literary, occupational specialization and target-seeking learning; instruction through ceremonials appears to occur in societies where more diffuse learning patterns are institutionalized (Henry, 1955a), together with highly structured personal communities (Henry, 1958). Ceremonial education seems to bring together two things: the responsibility of the broader kin group and the communication of knowledge.

In *The West African 'Bush' School*, Watkins (1943) describes aboriginal schools for boys and girls, conducted by secret societies and lasting from about two to eight years. The schools are isolated from the ongoing life of the tribe, and the buildings are destroyed when the session is over. There are separate schools for boys and girls. 'No one except members of the society is permitted entrance to the [school] area.' Among the Vai,

The principal official of the school is the *dá zò*: ... 'the leader who stands at the mouth or head', who is endowed with wisdom and mystic power in a superlative degree. He has a majestic status in the society [see III], is respected by the chief and elders of the tribe, and is honored with intense devotion by the youth of the land (pp. 668–9).

Among the Kpelle,

The grandmaster, *namu*, is, of course, a human being and is known as such by the members. At the same time he has attributes which raise him above the merely human (p. 669).

In these schools,

The boys are divided into groups according to their ages and apti-tudes and receive instruction in all the arts, crafts, and lore of native life. . . . The first instruction involves a series of tests in order to determine individual differences, interests, and ambitions. . . .

All this training is tested out in the laboratory of 'bush'-school life. For example, instruction in warfare is accompanied by actual mock battles and skirmishes. . . .

Life in the secret society is a complete *rite de passage* from the helplessness and irresponsibilities of childhood to citizenship in a world of adults. Thus a youth acquires a new name in the *beli*, according to his rank in the group of his achievements. . . . Entrance to the society is a symbolic death for the young, who must be reborn before returning to the family and kin. Those who die from the strenuous life are considered simply not to have been reborn, and their mothers are expected not to weep or grieve for them (pp. 670–71).

Here, then, is an entire area of the pre-literate world where there are schools similar in many ways to those of the literate world. It is hard to believe that these schools are not a combination of native initiation rituals and the white man's idea of a school.

II : 4. *By use of punishments;* II : 5. *By use of rewards*
In the *Ethica Nicomachea* (1925, p. 20), Aristotle says of pleasure that 'it is thought to be most intimately connected with our human nature, which is the reason why in educating the young we steer them by the rudders of pleasure and pain'. Since these are used consciously in education by all societies, it would seem that their use must reflect that 'psychic unity' of mankind of which anthropologists speak. II : 4 ('By use of punishments') does not refer merely to the use of pain as an accompaniment to learning (see II : 16 : (a)) but to the use of punishment as a means

of redirecting deviant behaviour. Similarly, II : 5 ('By use of rewards') refers to recognition of accomplishment, as when, for
example, adults in American society express to the child pleasure
at his mastery of language, walking, or going to the toilet instead
of wetting. When the Chagga (Raum, 1940, p. 135) tie little bells
to a baby's ankles to 'give him pleasure in stamping his feet so
that he may become steady on his legs', this is not reward in the
sense implied here. But if the mother hails the child's efforts to
walk with articulate joy, that is reward in the sense implied here.

One of the most interesting problems in education is the shift
that takes place from reward to conformity to mere punishment
for non-conformity as the child grows older; and the gradual
dropping out of rewards as the child's competence comes to be
taken for granted. One might hypothesize, for example, that the
American middle-class child who, let us say, is praised every time
he passes a 'dry night', might feel disappointed when his dryness
is taken for granted. On the other hand, he might feel insulted,
once dryness has been achieved, if he is still praised for something that any child of his age ought to be able to do. The problem may be summed up as follows: when a child has been
rewarded for his childish accomplishments, how does he feel
when these sources of recognition come to an end, especially
when he is then punished for his lapses?

II : 6. *Problem solving*
'Problem-solving' refers not to answering a question in arithmetic
or filling in a missing word in a sentence, but to analytico-
synthetic processes that bear on the logic of a situation. It is
closely related to the idea of decision-making. For example, there
is a story in an American fourth-year reader (Gray *et al.*, 1956) in
which a man and a boy are in a rowboat on the water when a fog
comes up. The boy knows the coast, but the man does not. The
man asks the boy to let him row, and the boy, just 'to be polite',
lets him, even though there is grave danger from rocks. Here a
problem would be: 'Did Andy do the right thing in letting the
man row?'

II : 7. *Guided recall*
'Guided recall' refers to the nearly universal procedure in American elementary and even high schools whereby the pupil is

guided by the teacher in recalling to mind the specific content of a lesson. With reference to the example in II : 6 above, guided recall would involve asking questions such as the following: 'Where were they?' ('Out in a boat.') 'What happened?' ('A fog came up.') 'Why was it dangerous?' ('Because of the rocks.') In guided recall, problem-solving opportunities in the lesson are not exploited.

II : 8. *Giving the child tasks to perform beyond his immediate capacity*

II : 8 : (a) Jamming the machine

Fortes says of education in Taleland that, 'A child is never forced beyond its capacity' (1938, p. 13). In American schoolrooms on the other hand, in spite of the ideology of 'readiness',* one observes a constant urging of children, sometimes to the limits of their capacity, toward a culturally determined standard of mastery. The result of this is that the learning 'machine' sometimes becomes 'jammed', and a child may, at that moment, be completely unable to perform. The following is an example from a fifth-grade class (Henry, 1955, p. 202):

The child at the board stares at $\frac{2}{3}$ minus $\frac{2}{3}$. There is a faint titter, snicker† giggle or something . . . as the child stares, nonplussed by the problem. The teacher goes up to her and demonstrates with a measuring cup: 'If we have $\frac{2}{3}$ of a cup here, and we pour it out, what is left?' The child remains baffled, and the teacher says it again, seeming to try to force her presentation of the problem on the child in such a way as to cut out the distracting influence of the class, which is eager to be helpful. Child finally says, 'Nothing,' and the teacher says, '*That's right.*'

In these contemporary schoolrooms, the child who says 'I can't' is urged until he can. As I read Fortes, I would interpret him to mean that, given a situation like the above, the Tale would let the child be, and try again a month or a year later. On the other hand, the Chagga (Raum, 1940) would appear to be much more determined than the Tale in their resolve to bring the child up

* The educational theory according to which all curricula should be carefully planned so that a student enters on each new subject matter and each advance in an old subject matter in terms of graduated steps that prepare him ('ready him') for the change.

† To *snicker* is to laugh in a sly, partly stifled manner.

as quickly as possible to a level of performance. The 'blackboard paralysis' we have seen above is a bio-social phenomenon that can occur only when there is a critical moment in the educational process at which massive pressures are brought to bear on a child to get him to perform an incompletely mastered task within a narrowly limited time. These are the conditions for what is here called 'jamming the machine'.

II : 10. *By kinaesthetic association*

By 'kinesthetic association' is meant the accompaniment of learning by gross muscular movement. Thus a Murngin boy (Warner, 1937) who executes a large number of ceremonial movements while he is learning the tribal traditions during initiation may tend to remember the traditions well because they have become associated to a complex series of physical manoeuvres. In the same way, a child in an American elementary school who paints a picture of some African scene when he is learning the geography of Africa may tend to remember his lesson well because the gross physical movements involved in painting become associated with the lesson. Finally, the child who goes through the *movements* of a play he enacts in connection with a lesson on Africa may tend to remember Africa not only because of the actual contents of the play but also because he has 'gone through' Africa with his body!

II : 12. *By doing*

'By doing' refers only to education in which the child learns a life-role by performing that role – for example, when a child learns to farm by cultivating the soil, or to fish by fishing. This contrasts with learning something *about* farming by reading on the life of a farmer. It does not include learning arithmetic by doing arithmetic, or learning reading by reading, etc.

II : 13. *By symbolic association*

The display of totemic emblems (Warner, 1937, p. 345) in an Australian initiation is education in basic tribal ideas concerning religion and social structure through symbolic association. The emblem is a symbol with which the boy associates the religious and socio-structural ideas. When a teacher in an American school draws a picture of a shamrock on the blackboard while she is talking about St Patrick's Day, this also is education through symbolic association. Another example is education of the Chinese boy in his ancestral traditions through showing him the clan books (Chiang, 1952, p. 9).

II : 14. *By dramatization*
Any act in which children dramatize a cultural fact is education through 'dramatization', whether it be ritual enactment in a ceremonial, or secular acting out of a story, as fourth-grade American children might act out the story of 'The Golden Pears' (Gray *et al.*, 1956).

II : 16 : (a). By trials
The use of physical trials or endurance tests as part of the educational process has had a wide vogue. Pettitt (1946) has documented this usage for the North American Indians. Raum (1940, pp. 205–208) says that at about twelve years of age Chagga boys are taught 'endurance and diligence' with the hoe, and that,

When the boy gets tired, he is threatened or beaten. The father scorns to take refreshment to him; this makes the boy's trial the more excruciating. Girls who hoe with their mothers are occasionally given something to nibble.
    [In learning how to plant bananas, the boy] sometimes has to carry a heavy plant for several miles, and begins to weep or ask permission to set his load down. His father tells him to bear up.

These excerpts from Raum illustrate not only II : 16 : (a) but also the use of physical force (II : 23), and the use of threats (II : 16), in education.
    The following from India illustrates another, apparently idiosyncratic, trial (Chaudhuri, 1951, p. 43):

I contracted a lifelong dislike for a most estimable relative of mine by being told that he was such a conscientious students that he never used the mosquito net, lest left in peace by the mosquitoes he might over-indulge himself in sleep, and also that before examinations he tied his legs with a rope to the beam so that, not being able to lie flat and in comfort on his bed, he might be cogitating his books in a state of half wakefulness.

11 : 17. *By irrelevant association;* II : 18. *By relevant association*
There is an American game called 'spelling baseball', for which

the children in a classroom are divided into two teams. The teacher gives each child in turn a word to spell, and, if it is spelled correctly, the child is credited with 'a hit' and goes to 'first base'. His next team-mate is given a word, and, if the team-mate is correct, he goes to first base and the first child moves to second base – and so on, until the team gets a 'run'. Each mis-spelled word is an 'out'. In this game, the competition runs high, and the children are nervously alert. Yet it is education through irrelevant association, because there is no connection between spelling and baseball : a perfectly illiterate man might make an excellent ballplayer. On the other hand, a game of 'cafeteria', in which the children play at being in a cafeteria, and having to spend money and figure the bill while making payment with toy money to a child appointed as cashier, is education through relevant association, because it is necessary to know how to count in order to buy in a real cafeteria, or in order to manage one. The American educational process does not reveal many exam-ples of education by irrelevant association, and our research has not uncovered any at all from other cultures.

II : 19. *Through art*

Education *through* art is not education *in* art.* Education through art is the issue here : it has to do with the use of artistic endeavour to facilitate the learning process. When children are being taught about Africa, and have an art period in which they draw or paint pictures of Africa, this is education through art; when they are having a lesson on 'Ireland and her neighbours', and sing songs from those countries, this too is education through art, for songs are an art form. Obviously, education through art can be considered from another point of view, i.e. the educating

---

* Most art lessons in American public schools are not lessons in art, for the reason that most teachers do not know how to teach art. The curriculum may produce art *periods*, during which the children paint or draw or cut out so-called 'abstractions', but the periods are usually not art *lessons*. The art periods in many school systems are merely minutes during which the children engage in some manual exercise prescribed by a routinized muni-cipal curriculum. During such moments, the children may make valentines, puppets, tiny woven mats to hold pots, etc., according to prescribed rules. Many teachers see the art period merely as a relaxation for the children, and only two of the regular teachers in our sample of several dozen seemed even to try to give any instruction in art at all.

of children through the use of artistic creations by others, such as plays or paintings. A good example is the play of Bali (Belo, 1919), which is at once artistic and educational. The Balinese plays are also entertaining. The American analogue, but on a much, much lower level almost wholly lacking in artistry, would be the pre-processed television cartoons that are used in some educational systems for teaching purposes. In this latter case, however, we are really dealing rather with II:9, education through the use of mechanical devices, rather than with education through art.

II : 24. *By positive or negative assertion*
Asking leading questions such as, 'We like rhyming words, don't we?' or making statements such as, 'The illustrations are very clever,' which the child is not expected to challenge, is what is implied by 'positive or negative assertion'. It would appear that what the teacher is aiming at by such verbalizations is student acquiescence-through-affirmation – a kind of acceptance-through-head-nodding. The *intent* of such verbalizations can be grasped if one tries to imagine any child saying, 'No, teacher, I hate rhyming words,' or, 'But really, teacher, I think the illustrations are terrible.'

II : 26. *By specifically relating information to the child's own*
        body, bodily function, or experience
Teachers in American elementary schools make broad use of the method of specifically relating information to the child's own body, bodily function, or experience. A reading lesson about pets will call forth from the teacher the question, 'Do any of you have pets?' A lesson on the functions of the body will lead the teacher to ask, 'What happens when you run?' ('We get out of breath.') Spiro (1958, p. 258) says of education in the *kibbutz*:

The teacher generally attempts to make the subject meaningful in terms of the child's own experiences and his immediate (physical or temporal) environment. In a fourth-grade art lesson, for example, the objects cast in plaster-of-Paris were animals and flowers with which the children were immediately familiar; in seeking for a subject for a drawing class shortly before the advent of Passover, the teacher suggested that the children draw a Passover scene. . . .

But the teacher attempts to relate the materials not only to the child's immediate experiences, but to his deepest interests as well. In a second-grade lesson in arithmetic, for example, the exercises in addition and subtraction were concerned with the winning and losing of marbles – an activity in which almost all the children were temporarily absorbed.

II : 27. *Through ego-inflation*

The method of 'ego-inflation' aims specifically at the child's conception of himself. A procedure, such as praise, for example, that enhances a child's opinion of himself or makes him feel appreciated, falls in this category. II : 27 *can* differ from II : 5 in that the latter can be mere recognition of a lesson well learned, as in the case of an American child who is permitted to use the family car when he has learned how to drive. II : 27, on the other hand, is aimed *specifically* at improving a child's opinion of himself. II : 27 and II : 5 may coincide in the same act, as in praise, for example.

II : 27 : (a). Through ego-deflation

A procedure, such as humiliation, for example, that diminishes the child's opinion of himself, falls in this category 'ego-deflation'.

II : 30. *By watching*

Probably all education involves some watching, but this category II : 30 attempts to capture that learning situation which is construed largely as one in which the learner learns primarily by watching. Thus Chiang says (1952, p. 58):

I do not remember that I ever had any proper lessons in painting from my father. He told me to watch him as closely as possible. . . . I remember that after watching my father painting a few times I thought I knew just how to paint, but when I actually began I found I was mistaken! . . . I asked my father to help, but he only smiled and told me to watch him again.

Fortes has the following to say about the Tale (1938, p. 13):

Rapid learning or the acquisition of a new skill is explained by *u mar nini pam*, 'he has eyes remarkably', that is, he is very sharp. A friend of mine who was a cap-maker told me how he learnt his craft, as a youth, from a Dagban by carefully watching him at work. When he was young, he explained, he had 'very good eyes'. This conception of cleverness is intelligible in a society where learning by looking and copying is the commonest manner of achieving dexterity both in crafts and in the everyday manual activities.

It is hard to find any conscious human learning that does not include all three processes of listening, watching and doing. Yet, it seems that cultures may differ in the degree to which one or the other is stressed, and in the degree to which one or the other is stressed in learning different *things*. Contemporary cultures, of course, have substituted reading for much of listening, and even of watching, since written directions accompanied by diagrams can replace watching. On the other hand, the American stress on 'learning by doing' suggests an 'action' approach to education. It seems possible that, while learning by doing may lead to an early mastery of, let us say, agricultural techniques, it may lead to a premature sense of mastery in painting, with consequent poor production. Belo and McPhee (Mead and Wolfenstein, 1954) have given us exciting materials on children's painting and music in Bali, but no description of the actual learning process. One of the puzzling problems in education is the exciting quality of children's painting and its disappearance in later life. What happens to all the budding artists? Why do they abandon their art altogether, or discard its most original dimensions – as in Bali, for example? One factor is suggested here: that children who learn by doing develop a premature sense of mastery, and that later comparison of their own work with that of a mature adult artist leads to destructive self-criticism. In offering this hypothesis I am not unaware of the importance of institutional supports for art. What place does a creative artist have in industrial culture, anyway? And what scope is there for originality in Bali? The answer in both cases is, *little*.

11 : 31. *By listening*

A great deal of learning involves listening, but this category II : 31 applies only to learning situations that are *defined* as listening ones. Thus Fortes quotes a Tale man as follows (1938: p. 12):

'If he listens will he not know, will he not acquire wisdom?' When children are very small. . . . they know nothing about religious things. 'They learn little by little. When we go to the shrine they accompany us and listen to what we say. Will they not [thus] get to know it? ... Whatever I do [my son] also sits and listents. Will he not get to know it thus?'

II : 32. *Question and answer*

The 'question and answer' method is so common in American culture that it is not easy for Americans to imagine another in which the child is expected, not to ask questions, but to learn by passively watching, listening, or copying. Yet, we have seen that the Chinese stress watching (see also II : 37) and that the Tale stress watching and listening. Among the Pilagá, the educational process includes a further interesting characteristic : Pilagá children learn a great deal simply by making incorrect statements that adults correct. For example, a child will point to an insect and give its name, and, if the name is incorrect, the adult will correct it.

II : 34. *By doing something on his own*

A child is said to be 'doing something on his own' when, for example, after he has asked, 'What makes clouds?' he follows an instruction to find the answer himself by going to an encyclopedia and other books on the subject. This category also covers the case of the Lepcha child who is given his own animals and plot of land to take care of (Gorer, 1938, pp. 108, 307).

II : 36. *By accusing*

'Young ears don't listen. Can't you look after your cattle properly, you good-for-nothings, you things-with-sunken-eyes ...' is one example, from Tale, of educating through accusation (Fortes, 1938, p. 14). It is also II : 27 : (a), education through ego-deflation.

II : 37. *By following a model*

When a teacher plays a song, or the first note of it, on a musical instrument, and children try to follow it, singing, this is following a non-human model (II : 37 : (b)). But when the teacher beats time with her arm for the children, this is following a human model (II : 37 : (a)). Again, when the teacher writes on a blackboard and the children try to copy her writing, this is following a human model. Any instance of a child's attempt to follow this kind of direction is considered to belong in II : 37. In Pettitt's language, it is 'directed practice'.

II : 38. By comparison

The category 'By comparison' has to do with those cases in which a child is educated through asking him to compare two or more objects, such as two lines of unequal length, or three colours like yellow, orange and chartreuse.

II : 39. By filling in a missing part

Teaching 'by filling in a missing part' is carried out by, for example, showing a child a book on language skills containing sentences with missing words and requiring him to fill in the missing words.

II : 43. Physical manipulation

II : 43 : (a). Bodily manipulation

Mead and Bateson (1942) afforded an example of 'bodily manipulation' in describing how children learn to dance in Bali: the child's body is against that of the instructor, and the two move in unison, the child learning how to dance partly through making his own movements coalesce with the instructor's.

Gorer (1938, p. 305) says the following of the Lepcha:

Children are taught work techniques by being instructed to copy their elders, by verbal admonition, or by having their arms held while they are put through the appropriate gestures.

II : 43 : (b). Bodily mutilation and other physical stresses

Bodily mutilation as an educational technique is common enough in primitive societies, and includes the piercing of lips and ears, removal of teeth, scarification, circumcision, sub-incision, and clitterodectomy. It would appear that man early made the discovery that, within limits, learning would be most strongly reinforced in the presence of anxiety, hence the inclusion of bodily mutilation in many tribal rituals in which fundamental tribal lore is taught to young men or women. The relation between mutilation and learning has many complexities, as can be seen, e.g. from the following about the Chagga (Raum, 1940, p. 311):

That the parental generation regards circumcision, not only as a test, but as an opportunity for cumulative punishment appears from the fact that any notorious mischief-monger is submitted to a severe trial. His circumcision is attended by those of his elders who bear a grudge against him. When the operator has made the preliminary incision, he is told to stop. Someone steps on the victim's big toe to find out whether he squirms and to beat him if he does. He is told to sing a song without hesitating or trembling. After some other boys have been circumcised, the operator is allowed to continue on the culprit, but before he is finished he is told: 'Leave him for another while!' Only after a lengthy interval is the operation completed. In some cases a boy is under the knife for an hour or longer. The report of this torture is spread among the uncircumcised and stupefies them with terror. In consequence they willingly obey and honour their elders. . . .

Here the Chagga have contrived that circumcision shall be an *anticipated* threat, so that the ensuing anxiety may provide a motivation for learning. Circumcision, a physical stress, is accompanied by emotional stress.

The Chagga case opens up the general problem of the introduction of stress into the educational process. Pettitt (1946, p. 89) has the following to say about the functions of stress in the education of some North American Indians:

The point to be made is that in the vision quest [a major educational experience] . . . the objective was . . . to produce an independent, self-confident, and self-reliant personality, buoyed up by an inner conviction of his ability to meet any and all situations. . . . The painful ordeals . . . strengthened his character, and supplied him with experience in withstanding physical suffering, which was . . . important in giving him self-assurance. . . .

Pettitt, abstracting from Teit's numerous publications on the Thompson River Indians of British Columbia, describes the Thompson River Indian boy's vision quest as follows (1946, pp. 87–8):

When a boy's dream became propitious . . . his vision quest began in earnest. As a ceremonial beginning, he was required to run, with bow and arrows in his hands, until bathed in perspiration and on the point of exhaustion, when he was made to plunge in cold water. This was repeated four times a day for four days . . . Although his first four days were consumed in running and bathing, the first four nights were given to dancing, singing and praying, with little or no sleep, around a fire on some near-by mountain peak. . . .

Having acted out the prologue, the boy then began work in

earnest. He went on lonely pilgrimages into the mountains, staying away from home and eating nothing for from four to eight days on end. It was a common practice to schedule these pilgrimages in winter, so that the boy would not be tempted by berries and roots. During these vigils the boy usually took nothing with him but a fire drill and a sleeping mat. He intensified the effect of his fasting by taking herbal concoctions with a purgative action, and by poking long twigs down his throat until he vomited. ... The boy continued this exhausting regime until he had a dream of some animal or bird which would be his protector through life.

Pettitt summarizes also (1946, p. 101) some of Stern's material on the Lumi Indians of the Pacific Northwest of North America:

The first objective of training is to give the boy confidence and make him fearless. He is sent out on dark stormy nights to perform trumped-up errands, such as fetching a bow or some other article from a friend or relative living at some distance ... The status of childhood is made uncomfortable by depriving him of the best foods, discriminating against him, making him bathe in cold water, morning and night. At the slightest breach of this discipline, which he knows will end when he proves his manhood, his father becomes enraged, and may throw burning bark in his face. As he grows older the rigor of his regime increases. He is instructed to rub his body with cedar bark to toughen his muscles. His father tests his stamina from time to time by cutting gashes in his body, starting with the more calloused parts and working up to the more tender. He is stimulated to greater efforts by the warning that he will turn into a girl unless he watches out. In fact, these warnings are often taken so seriously that a boy rubs his breasts with sand until they bleed, or smashes the nipples between rocks to stop a fancied over-development.
    Finally, he is ready to make his quest. He goes to some secluded spot and seeks by his endurance to out-strip all other boys of whom he has heard, thereby winning the favour of the supernaturals. ... If rocks assume strange shapes in the darkness, he must stand his ground, in fact run toward them and grapple with them ... The boy may stay away from his village for a year or even four years ... through living alone he builds up a sense of self-sufficiency.

Thus, through isolation (see II:55) and the self-imposition of various austerities, the boy made himself physically and emotionally capable of withstanding pain, hunger and thirst in later

life. What happened, in addition, was an orientation of the personality away from childish things, a hardening of determination,
and, most importantly, a consolidation of the culturally requisite
conceptions of the world – in Radcliffe-Brown's terminology, a
crystallization of the 'collective sentiments'.

Among the Tiwi of North Australia, physical and emotional
stresses are combined in the educational process in a different
way. There, initiation is taken over by persons who are strangers
to the boy. This in itself is frightening to him, but, in addition,
the way in which the strangers appear on the scene is terrifying.
Hart describes this vividly (1955, pp. 134–5):

Among the Tiwi of North Australia, one can see the traumatic nature
of the initiation period in very clear form, and part of the trauma lies
in the sudden switch of personnel with whom the youth has to associate. A boy reaches thirteen or fourteen or so, and the physiological
signs of puberty begin to appear. Nothing happens, possibly for
many months. Then suddenly, one day towards evening when the
people are gathering around their campfires for the main meal of the
day after coming in from their day's hunting and food-gathering, a
group of three or four heavily armed and taciturn strangers appear in
camp. In full war regalia they walk in silence to the camp of the boy
and say curtly to the household: 'We have come for So-and-So.'
Immediately pandemonium breaks loose. The mother and the rest
of the older women begin to howl and wail. The father rushes for his
spears. The boy himself, panic-stricken, tries to hide, the younger
children begin to cry, and the household dogs begin to bark. . . .
    The father's rush for his spears . . . is make-believe. . . . With the
father immobilized the child clings to his mother, but the inexorable
strangers soon tear him (literally) from his mother's arms . . . and,
still as grimly as they came, bear him off into the night. No society
could symbolize more dramatically that initiation necessitates the
forcible taking away of the boy from the bosom of his family, his
village, his neighbours, his intimates, his friends.

While Hart needlessly generalizes the use of force, and over-
estimates the extent to which in other parts of the primitive world
education is shifted at puberty from intimates to strangers, the
fright of the boys and the mock battle staged by their fathers are
described by Warner (1958, p. 261), with variations, also for the
Murngin, another Australian tribe. The point is that the initia-

tion begins with massive fright stimuli which are repeated at strategic moments during the ceremony (see, for example, Warner, 1958, p. 282). Presumably their function is to force a reorientation of the boys' personalities.

It has been pointed out that education always involves a narrowing of the perceptual field to the universe selected by the culture. It has also been suggested that narrowing occurs partly through emphasizing only that cultural universe. But the important question then is: how is that cultural universe emphasized? Some answers to this question have been suggested in section II. For example, punishment for straying from cultural norms, and reward for consistently practising them, are obvious devices for narrowing the perceptual field to the desired universe.

It would appear from the primitive North American, Australian, and Chagga data, that the massive application of pain to, and provocation of anxiety and other stresses in, primitive boys during periods of great solemnity, would serve, in general, to narrow the perceptual sphere. The Chagga technique of making circumcision an implied threat (II : 15) is a good example of a special use of anxiety for this purpose: any indulgence before initiation in behaviours not sanctioned by the elders might result in torture at initiation.

In American public schools there are no physical stresses comparable to those experienced by the Chagga, by the North American Indians, or by the Australians. Emotional stresses are, nevertheless, constantly operative in American classrooms. Outstanding, of course, is the ever-present fear of failure, which tends to make the student accept almost any idea. There are, in addition, more specific techniques for fixing cultural configurations in the student's mind, like teaching by holding up adult ideals (II : 21), by having the children act in undifferentiated unison (II : 22), and by using positive or negative assertion (II : 24). For example, if the child has held up before him certain adult ideals as he acts in undifferentiated unison with a group of his peers, the emotional impact will reinforce commitment to the culture. The method of positive or negative assertion, II : 24, is a kind of implied threat, which seems to say, 'If you do not like [whatever the teacher wants you to like], you probably have something wrong with you; so you had better learn to like it.' With respect to using ego-inflation (II : 27) or ego-deflation (II : 27 : (a)), it seems likely that since a cultural experience that enhances the self-image will be rewarding, such an experience will serve to anchor the components of that experience in the child's personality; while, on the other hand, ridicule or contempt accompanying failure may make the child struggle hard to succeed. Of course, the experience may have the opposite effect, thereby laying the basis for culture conflict and change. This is true also of II : 4, using punishment.

Before closing this section, it is necessary to indicate that there seem to be some physical stresses accompanying education, especially in literate cultures, which tend to act in an inhibitory way on some aspects of learning, perhaps while reinforcing others. For example, long hours spent sitting in one spot might render students antagonistic to subject matter but teach them self-control. This suggests that the imposition of such physical restrictions during education would be a screening device through which only the culturally most desirable persons could pass, i.e. those who could combine attention to subject matter with self-control. Thus all the rules of order in school, to the degree that they govern physical behaviour, are, along with the curriculum, mechanisms for separating the children into good learners and poor ones.

As one glances over this list of educational methods that is section II, one cannot but be struck by their mere number. The reason for the number is that since humans have no innate techniques of adaptation to the environment, including culture, they have to learn them. The problem for *homo sapiens* was twofold, for not only was the *acquisition* of knowledge through learning essential to his adaptation, but he had also to devise *methods* of teaching what he knew to his offspring. Thus a further problem arose out of his necessity for devising different methods for teaching different bodies of knowledge. The result was a lengthening list of teaching methods as knowledge increased.

The length of the list raises a general question as to the relation between number of methods and level of cultural complexity. Some answer to this question has been attempted (Henry, 1955a, pp. 199–202), and the suggestion made that, as the number of cultural items to be learned increases, the number of teaching methods increases also, but that the time expended to educate about each item probably fluctuates too (see section XII, p. 176). Actually, what we seem to have in contemporary American culture, as compared with primitive societies, is a greater number of teaching methods, less time allotted to each subject taught, but an enormous amount of time spent in formal instruction. Meanwhile, the American child is repeatedly placed in the position of having his 'machine jammed' (II:8:(a)). Jamming the machine is so characteristic of contemporary culture because, given the enormous amount of learning expected of a child, there has not been sufficient improvement in teaching methods, even though the catalogue of them seems extensive. Modern man's inventiveness of cultural content appears to have outstripped his ingenuity in devising methods to communicate that content. Students whose failure compels them to drop out of school or curtail their schooling are thus, in part, casualties of cultural lag – of the failure of teaching methods to keep pace with content.

III. WHO EDUCATES?

III : 1. *Males or females?*
The revolutionary change in the United States from male to female teachers occurred in the 1860s during and after the Civil War. Even before this, American women had been breaking the socio-economic taboos that blocked their entrance into the labour force, but with the increased use of women workers by the government and the rapid expansion of American industry after the war, with consequent more lucrative opportunities available to men, women began to flock into the educational system (Calhoun, 1945, vol. 2, pp. 359–61). At the same time, the curriculum became a 'common gender' curriculum – not 'masculine' or 'feminine'. That is to say, the American public-school curriculum became more and more shaped to fit the requirements of both males and females rather than of males only. Thus there is a relationship in the United States between the development of a common-gender curriculum and the lack of sexual specialization in teaching: though most elementary-school teachers in America are females, males are very much desired and they are heavily represented in high schools and colleges.

III : 2. *Relatives or others?*
Another feature of pre-literate education has been the concentration within the kin group of responsibility for educating the young (Fortes, 1938, p. 5). The child's mother's brother and father's sister (Pettitt, 1946, pp. 15-24) have often assumed this responsibility. Meanwhile, there appears to be a systematic relationship between the content of education at any given moment and the kin category, or categories, that assumes responsibility for it (Henry, 1955, pp. 191-2). One of the commonest is the responsibility of the same-sex parent for training in occupational techniques, and the responsibility of the wider kin group for training in morality. In contemporary America, neither schools nor parents are required by law to teach morality, though the social conscience still expects parents to assume this responsibility. Occupational training, on the other hand, has been handed over to non-kin agencies, the reverse of the more ancient cultural pattern.

III : 3. *On which age group does the burden of education fall?*
III : 3 : (a) Peers
Many references to peer education are scattered through Fortes's penetrating study (1938). In this respect, Chagga boys emphasize masculinity (Raum, 1940, p. 211). Egyptian boys are sensitive to standards of 'maturity', and are bitterly scornful of a boy whose behaviour does not come up to his age level (Ammar, 1954, p. 128). But the educational responsibilities that children's peer groups had in pre-literate and peasant cultures have tended to diminish with the emergence of the common-gender curriculum, the approximation of male and female roles, and the handing over of occupational training to non-kin.

Peer education seems most prominent at all cultural levels in the area of conformity to cultural standards. In pre-literate and peasant societies, the peer group is a major force against delinquency. In contemporary society, the peer group seems split on this issue: it is a major support of rebellion against parents (and hence of the cultural standards they represent), while, at the same time, it does use its power to assist conformity to accepted adult standards of morality (Hollingshead, 1949). It would seem that this capacity to take rebellion as a standard of conformity to peer-group mores is related to the fact that *in the long run* children in contemporary culture will not, as in many peasant and pre-literate cultures, receive their economic foundation in life from their parents.

III : 4. *Is education by 'successful' people?* III : 5. *What rewards accrue to the educator?*

The categories 'Is education by "successful" people?' and 'What rewards accrue to the educator?' are closely related. For example, Williams (1949, vol. 1, p. 426) says of Chinese teachers that they are 'unsuccessful students or candidates for literary degrees' but that, nevertheless, 'When a boy comes to school in the morning he bows first before the tablet of Confucius, as an act of worship, and then salutes his teacher . . .' for the teacher taught the sacred writings of Confucius and his disciples. Chiang (1952, pp. 79–82) tells about the reverence with which his teacher was treated and the absolute authority over the children granted him by parents. Thus there has been no necessary connection between success, as measured by worldly standards, and the *deference* accorded a teacher (III : 5 : (a), (c)). In the *shtetl* (Zborowski and Herzog, 1952, p. 89) the *melamed*, the teacher of the youngest children, was looked down upon as a man who, because 'he has fallen into his profession because he has failed elsewhere', is driven to sell what should be given freely, i.e. learning. Nevertheless, his word was law in the school, and there was no appeal to parents from his cruelty. In eighteenth-century Germany (Bruford, 1935, pp. 247–50), teachers were of low status and were often treated like servants. In nineteenth-century England (Bayne Powell, 1939, p. 69), the outstanding requirement in schoolmasters was 'humility', and they were 'despised'. In Egypt, on the other hand, the sheikhs were accorded great deference, a function of the fact that 'they are the perpetuators of the Holy Book' (Ammar, 1954, p. 211). From all of this, four factors seem to emerge. 1. There is no necessary connection between the success of a teacher according to worldly standards and the deference granted to him. 2. There is no necessary connection between the deference granted a teacher and the authority he, compared with parents, wields over children. 3. There seems to be a connection between the sacredness of knowledge and the deference accorded a teacher in the community as a whole. 4. Europe and the United States have a recorded history of low esteem for schoolteachers.

In the light of the foregoing, we can obtain some understanding of the reason for the poor pay received by American teachers. The low esteem in which teachers have been traditionally held in the United States continues today (Kahl, 1957, p. 73), and low esteem is usually accompanied by low pay. It is further suggested that the reason for the disdain of teachers is the detachment of American education from the 'sacred' (Durkheim, 1947), i.e. the lack of any deeply felt social consciousness of the aims of education.

III : 8. *Is the educator of the same or of a different social group from that of the person being educated?*
The issue of coincidence or lack of coincidence between the social group of the educator and of the educated of course vigorously confronts anthropology in situations of acculturation, but, since it constitutes a chapter by itself in the history of education, it will be barely touched on here. Malinowski (1943, pp. 649–65) has discussed the issue with insight and feeling in connection with Africa, pointing out that missionary education 'undermined and destroyed' the native culture, while holding out a promise of equality with Europeans that was, however, not kept. Thompson (1943, p. 720) says that a committee appointed to inquire into British educational policy in Ceylon found that the policy there had done nothing more than produce

a class of shallow, conceited, half-educated youths who have learned nothing but to look back with contempt upon the conditions in which they were born and from which they conceive that their education has raised them, and who desert the ranks of the industrious classes to become idle, discontented hangers-on of the courts and the public offices.

In the United States, arbitrary efforts to educate Indians along lines laid down by the federal government's Office of Indian Affairs had for many years an inglorious outcome. Macgregor (1946) concentrating on the disastrous consequences for Dakota Indian children, emphasizes (1946, pp. 434–37): 1. the children's fright at encountering large numbers of strange children in the government boarding schools maintained for Indians; 2. fear, by these non-competitive Indian children, of the competitive situation created by the white schoolteachers; 3. fear of white teachers because whites had always been looked upon as enemies of the Indian; 4. severity of school discipline as contrasted with the more permissive atmosphere of Indian family life; 5. linguistic difficulties, so that many children could not even understand 'the teacher's simplest directions'. As a consequence, many children 'refuse to enter into competition, withdraw from activities, and sometimes become unwilling to make any response'. Children would withdraw into themselves or run away from school. They were often overwhelmed with shame when they could not win in a given situation. Leighton and Kluckhohn (1948) discuss similar conditions in Navaho schools.

Study of these and similar situations, and Hollingshead's study (1949) of the relation between social class and education in a small American city, document the fact that a controlling social group, whether it be whites over Negroes (Warner, Havighurst and Loeb (1944), whites over Indians (Macgregor, 1946), a colonial power over its colonial peoples (Malinowski, 1943; Thompson, 1943), or the higher classes over the lower (Hollingshead, 1919), tends to organize the educational system so as to strengthen and maintain its own position.

The works of anthropologists tend to stress the repressive and destructive effects on the subordinate group of education by the dominant group. Malinowski (1943), however, though giving the white man's education of the African little quarter, mentions that missionary education did start the African on the way toward dealing with the new civilization. Sometimes subordinate peoples exposed to modern education have extracted benefits from it, ranging from increased capacity to earn a living in the modern milieu, to the ability to engineer and sustain a social revolution, as in contemporary Africa. Leonard and Loomis (1911) have shown that while education of Spanish-Americans by Spanish-American teachers in New Mexico accomplished little because of the teachers' poor training, Spanish-American boys enrolled in Civilian Conservation Corps and National Youth Administration camps run by non-Spanish-Americans emerged well trained in reading, writing, and other academic skills and returned to their native towns with enhanced status.

IV. How does the person being educated
participate? (what is his attitude?)

All the following attitudes of children toward education are
known exclusively from literate cultures: 'rejecting: resistive'
(IV:2), 'bored; indifferent' (IV:3), 'defiant' (IV:4), 'inattentive' (IV:5), 'diversion to peers' (IV:27), 'disruptively' (IV:33).
These seem to stem most generally from the child's failure to feel
an immediacy in the relation between what is being taught him in
school and the rest of his life. Studies of education in pre-literate
cultures emphasize that knowledge is *sought* as a guide to an
inevitable life-role. This contrasts, as Mead (1943) has pointed
out, with literate cultures, where the child is subjected to com-
pulsory education but may not see its relevance to his future
role as an adult, or to his immediate life outside of school. More
concretely, in non-literate cultures the child is always in close
physical contact with the matured activity that he is merely
learning. In literate cultures, the school itself, and what he is
learning in it, are physically separate from adult *application* of
the learning: offices and other places where writing and arithmetic are *used* separate from the school where the child is learning how to read and add.

Spiro was struck by the apparent boredom, indifference and
inattention, of many children in the *kibbutz* high school (1958,
pp. 296–7):

Taking a random sample of twenty-four observational protocols, we
rated the students' apparent interest on a simple interested disinterested dichotomy. Lively group participation, careful attention,
intelligent questions, and so on, were taken as indications of interest,
while such statements in the protocols as: 'The children looked
bored and sleepy'; 'They daydream, doodle, play with objects in their
desks ...'; 'The children are apathetic and listless: they do not
participate in the discussion. They look bored. At least three heads
on the desks'; ... [etc.] were taken as indications of disinterest. On
the basis of these simple criteria, fifteen of the twenty-four sessions
were judged to elicit the students' interest, and nine were rated as
sessions in which they were disinterested or bored.

It seems likely that in the *kibbutz* this behaviour stems from the
same factors as in other literate cultures.

IV : 6. *Social closeness of teacher and child;* **IV : 7** *Social distance of teacher and child*

Spiro (1958, p. 263) ascribes 'informality' in the *kibbutz* primary school largely to the lack of 'social distance' between teacher and children: the children know the teacher personally, and see her in many roles outside of school. 'Social closeness' is thus viewed in terms of long-standing continuous interaction. But the term may be used also to describe less permanent interactional situations, as in American classrooms, where the children see the teacher only during class periods. In the American classroom, social distance may be gauged in terms of certain kinds of behaviour peculiar to the classroom, that is, the following categories in section **IV**:

IV : 15. *Through making independent decisions and suggestions*
 17. *Through spontaneous contributions or other demonstrations not precisely within the context of the lesson*
 18. *Through spontaneous contributions within the context of the lesson*
 20. *Spontaneously humorous*
 21. *Spontaneously expressive*
 22. *Approaches teacher physically*
 23. *Mobile – free*
 32. *Corrects teacher*
 45. *Uses teacher's first name*
 46. *Calls out to teacher*

That is to say, the extent to which children make independent decisions and offer suggestions to an adult mentor regarding the conduct of a lesson or other activity, the level of general mobility or of approach to the teacher's person, and the frequency with which children call out to the teacher and use his first name (rare in American culture outside the nursery school) all bear upon social distance. This term refers to a bundle of behaviours that are related to how secure, relaxed and accepted children seem to feel in a teacher's presence, and he in theirs.

Since the children's behaviour occurs in interaction with the teacher, it is necessary at this point to consider the relevance of these categories in section **IV** to certain categories in section **V**.

In section V – 'How Does the Educator Participate? (What is His Attitude?)' – the categories most relevant to the problem of social distance would appear to be:

4(a). Integrative
  7. *Enjoys correct response*
 10. *Seeks physical contact with person being educated*
 11. *Acceptance of blame*
 14. *Encouraging*
 16. *Relatively mobile*
 18. *Personalizing*
 21. *Accepts approach*
 23. *Accepting of child's spontaneous expressions*
 25. *Humorous*
 26. *Handles anxiety, hostility, discomfort, etc.*
 27. *Acts and/or talks as if child's self-image is fragile*
 29. *Defends child against peers*
 30. *Responds to non-verbal cue other than hand-raising*

That is to say, when American *children* display behaviours indicating their feeling of social closeness to the teacher, the American teacher will probably be found to be 'integrative'. He will show pleasure at correct responses, occasionally pat a child, be encouraging, move about the room, make frequent use of the children's names, let them come close to him, accept outbursts of joy, sorrow, or anxiety, deal appropriately with emotional problems as they arise, be sensitive to the children's feelings, defend a child who comes under verbal or physical attack by another child, and be perceptive enough of cues emanating from the children so that he will respond to frowns, smiles, tenseness, etc. – in other words, not wait for a question or a raised hand before responding. Thus social closeness can be expressed as a pattern of classroom behaviours quite apart from whether the children see the teacher after class periods.

Spiro describes *kibbutz* behaviours that in American schools would also indicate closeness (1958, p. 261):

Students leave the classroom at will – to get a drink, to go to the toilet, or for any reason which they deem important. Similarly, they may leave their desks without permission – to get supplies from the cabinet, to sharpen a pencil, and so on.

They may talk among themselves [IV:27] both during oral lessons and while working privately at their desks; some hum or sing to themselves while writing or studying.

A second expression of informality is readiness of the children to criticize the teacher when they feel he is wrong.

Students ... address their teachers by their first names and the latter address their students as chaverim, 'comrades'. ...

The *kibbutz* is much more tolerant of random behaviour than the American classrooms studied :

A final expression of classroom informality is the poor discipline. ... particularly in the second through fourth grades in the primary school, and the eighth through tenth grades in the high school – and which often results in utter chaos (Spiro, 1958 p. 261).

Such behaviour would be considered '*disruptive*' (IV : 33) in most American classrooms, though Henry (1959) has described occasional approval of it in suburban schools. Spiro (1958, p. 263) feels that this extreme informality is due to lack of social distance between teacher and child : yet, though in primitive cultures the social distance between teacher and pupil is, with certain exceptions (Watkins, 1943), very small, I have not found in primitive culture such generalized random behaviour *when the children are receiving systematic instruction in cultural skills*. The most general explanation of the occurrance of random behaviour is that adults permit it – if, indeed, they do not encourage it – by failure, as in the *kibbutz* and in some American suburban schools, to establish a clear locus of authority. Both in the United States and in the *kibbutz*, this is an expression of special interpretation of democracy. On the other hand, in the suburban American schools studied by Henry (1959), the chaos itself seems to be a value; random behaviour is believed to be creative behaviour. Finally, it is likely that lack of unity in the social sphere makes its contribution to unruliness, for when children do not see the relevance to their life-roles of what they are doing, boredom and inattention (IV : 3, 5) may ensue.

IV : 11. *With inappropriate laughter*

'Inappropriate laughter' signifies laughter that occurs in a context not socially defined as humorous, or laughter that is not part of a formal sanction pattern. The following from an American fifth-grade schoolroom is illustrative :

The child at the board stares at $\frac{2}{3}$ minus $\frac{2}{3}$. There is a faint titter, snicker, giggle or something. ... as the child stares, nonplussed by the problem.

Also illustrative is the following from a spelling lesson in a fourth-grade class:

The child writing 'Thursday' on the board stops to think after the first letter, and the children snicker. He stops after another letter. More snickers.

At the same time, it is not quite correct to say that failure is not 'socially defined' as humorous *by the children*; or that, for children in American society, laughter at failure is not part of the *children's* formal sanction pattern. Since it occurs to frequently among children in our research, it must be assumed to be a sanction within the children's group, and therefore, to be inappropriate only from the adult point of view. This does not mean that adults in American society do *not* take pleasure in other people's failure (Henry, 1957a).

IV : 11 : (a). Ridiculing peers
Ridicule is closely related to laughter as a social sanction against those who fail to come up to cultural demands. Pettitt says ridicule is 'world-wide in distribution' (1946, p. 50), and makes the important observation (1946, p. 53) that in primitive North America 'ridicule follows and supplements praise rather than vice versa. Praise is more frequently used at all age levels, and the ratio of praise to ridicule is relatively greatest at the younger ages.' The materials from contemporary American public grade schools do not parallel those from primitive North America. Our records show that, in American primary public schools, children do praise one another's work, but that ridicule, as expressed in spontaneous tittering, is more frequent. On the other hand, it is rare to find in these schools a ridiculing *teacher*, or one who laughs at the failure of one of her students.

The impression one derives from the literature on both literate and non-literate cultures is that ridicule is more common within the peer groups than across age lines, and that it is less common for a younger person to use it towards an older person that the reverse. This latter is understandable since the younger is more often the subordinate both in learning situations and with respect to the sanction system.

Among the numerous penetrating insights in Pettitt's work is his observation that ridicule did not occur in a random way among the Indians of North America. He says that 'the right to ridicule with impunity was generally limited', and that there was usually a 'privileged' group of ridiculers (like certain relatives) for every person (1946, pp. 50–52). Thus ridicule, probably because of its damage to the self-image and its great potential for generating hostility, was strictly controlled. There is no doubt that the importance of controlling ridicule was a brilliant psychological discovery by primitive man, and one wonders, therefore, why, once he had made that one, he did not go on to further triumphs. Speaking impressionistically again, it seems that they did, but that we need another Pettitt to comb the literature to find them, for these discoveries occurred in a scattered, unsystematized way, some in one tribe, some in another.

IV : 13. *Overt docility*
Ammar says of education in Egypt (1954, p. 127):

The keynote to the educational process is the eagerness of the adults to create a docile attitude in their children and thus make them acquire filial piety. The children readily accept the authority of their seniors, whether in work or play, and they endeavour to avoid their anger.

This is *not* the type of docility to which IV:13 refers. Henry (1955a) describes 'overt docility' as a child's renunciation of his own ideas in order to please the teacher. Two examples from a fourth-grade class in an American public school will illustrate the point:

During the art lesson Mrs Mintner holds up a picture and says, 'Isn't Bobby getting a nice effect of moss and trees?' The children utter ecstatic Ohs and Ahs.

The children have just finished reading the story of *The Sun, Moon, and Stars Clock* (Savery, 1942) and Mrs Mintner asks them, 'What was the highest point of interest, the climax?' The children tell her what they think it is. The teacher is aiming to get from them what she thinks it is, but the children give everything else but the answer she wants. At last Tom says, 'When they capture the thieves,' and Mrs Mintner asks, 'How many agree with Tom?' A great flurry of hands goes up.

IV : 20. *Disjoined hand-raising*
'Disjoined hand-raising' has been discussed at some length under I : 10 : (b) ('Use of the mind disjunction'). The 'disjoined hand' is the hand that is kept raised for no objective reason : the teacher has asked no question, nor created any other situation that calls for hand-raising, but the child's hand is up because he is detached from the situation and does not know what is going on.

IV : 34 *By carping criticism*
Henry (1957a) has discussed the phenomenon of 'Carping criticism' in public elementary-school classrooms. Carping criticism ignores the virtues in a work and concentrates destructively on petty details. For example, when a student reads to the class a little story he has composed, his classmates may ignore the good things in the story and pick out insignificant items to devalue. Often this occurs as a miscarriage of the idea that children should be taught to think 'critically', the teacher herself inadvertently starting criticism of this kind (see V : 36).

Carping criticism does not appear to occur in *kibbutz* schools :

The emphasis on group criticism can potentially engender competitive, if not hostile feelings among the children. Frequently, for example, the children read their essays aloud, and the others are then asked to comment. Only infrequently could we detect any hostility in the criticisms of the students, and often the evaluations were filled with praise (Spiro 1958, p. 261).

Thus, *kibbutz* children show more IV : 35 ('Praising work of peers') that IV : 34; and this is probably related to their great group solidarity within a markedly cooperative social structure.

IV : 37. *Attempts to maintain order*
In some suburban schools in the United States, where the ideology of permissiveness has penetrated deeply so that the classroom becomes very noisy, the tolerance limits for disorder are at times passed for some children, and they spontaneously 'Shush!' (i.e. to quiet) their peers. This exemplifies what is meant by 'Attempts to maintain order', and raises the interesting problem

of the tolerance of different children for disorder. In the language of communications theory, the question would be, 'How much noise can different persons tolerate in the communications system before the messages coming to them become completely blurred?' The problem of motivation is also involved here, for some children might not care how much noise there is in the system because they are not interested in the messages anyway. From the standpoint of the teacher, the issue would seem to be, 'How much noise can a child tolerate in the communications system before messages are lost to him or before he feels incapable of competing with the noise?' These problems have been taken up by Henry (1955a).

IV : 42. *Attempts to control the class*
The category 'Attempts to control the class' differs from 'Attempts to maintain order' (IV : 37) in that its referent is not the teacher but the child. The focus is not on a teacher's efforts to maintain order, but rather on one child's efforts to get other children in the educational situation to do what he wants them to do. An example from a fourth-grade class in singing will illustrate the point:

The children are singing songs from Ireland and her neighbours. . . . While the children are singing some of them hunt in the index of the song book, find a song belonging to one of the countries, and then raise their hands before the previous song is finished, in order that they may choose the next song to be sung. The index gives the national origin of each song.

When, in this situation, the teacher calls on a child whose hand is raised and accepts his selection of a song, the child has controlled the other children, because they have to sing his song. This category differs also from III : 3 : (a), 'Peer-group responsibility for education', because in the latter we are concerned only with whether or not instruction is given by the peer group, whereas in IV : 42 we are interested in whether or not a child attempts to impose his will on a learning group.

V. How does the educator participate?
(what is his attitude?)

V: 1. *Eagerly*

No anthropologist has ever asked whether adults in non-literate societies enjoy teaching. This must be because instructing the young in the tribal ways is as natural as breathing; the adults have a vital interest in the children they teach, and they often seem to have even a broader interest in the tribal existence as a whole. While Dubois (1944) and Raum (1940) give some evidence to show that children outside of Western culture can be reluctant to learn what they are supposed to learn, the overall impression gained from reading the literature on non-literate cultures is that children appear to want to learn tribal ways, and that adults take the children's role as learners, and their own as educators, for granted. But this is only impression, for anthropology has not explored systematically the problem of the eagerness of the primitive teacher to teach, or, indeed, of the primitive child to learn.

In contemporary culture, teachers have no kinship or other compelling motivations for eagerness in their work, and there arises in the study of classroom learning the problem of discovering whether such a teacher enjoys his occupation and whether he demonstrates it in class. It is suggested that observations focused on the sub-categories under V: 1 in the outline, and on the following group of categories indicating social closeness, would cast light on this matter:

V: 4(a). Integrative

7. *Enjoys correct response*

10. *Seeks physical contact with person being educated*

16. *Relatively mobile*

18. *Personalizing*

21. *Accepts approach*

22. *Repels approach*

25. *Humorous*

26. *Handles anxiety, hostility, discomfort, etc.*

27. *Acts and / or talks as if child's self-image is fragile*

30. *Responds to non-verbal cue other than hand-raising*

V: 11. *Acceptance of blame*

The category 'Acceptance of blame' would seem to apply more to literate than to non-literate cultures, and is particularly rele-

vant in the kind of 'democratic' classroom atmosphere peculiar
to the United States. The category would cover a situation where
something goes wrong in the conduct of the lesson, the children
tell the teacher it is his fault, and he accepts the blame.

V : 12. *Putting decisions up to the children*
Spiro (1958, p. 264) describes decision making in the *kibbutz*
school as follows:

The teacher, furthermore, generally consults with his students, rather
than informing them of decisions he had made independently. Even
in the grammar school, for example, the teacher chooses a project
only after consultation with the class. It is true that she presents
them with the suggestions from which a project is to be chosen, but
the final choice rests on the decision of the class. An even more
'democratic' procedure is adopted with respect to the writing of
essays for which the children themselves suggest the topics.

In this type of situation where the teacher puts decisions up to
the children, there is always the problem of whether such action
by the teacher is democratic or *pseudo*-democratic. In *pseudo-*
democratic action, the teacher, by suggestion or by limitation of
the area of selection, can actually bind the act of choice while
making it appear that it has been free. Henry (1959) has described such a situation in one American elementary school where
a teacher said his children themselves set up the behaviour rules,
but where, actually, they did so under his direction, to that the
rules were in the end what he wanted them to be. Placing decision making in the hands of the children is not characteristic
of American public elementary schools. Even cases of pseudo
democracy, such as that described by Henry, would appear to be
infrequent.

V : 18. *Personalizing*; V : 19. *Depersonalizing*
The categories 'Personalizing' and Depersonalizing' refer largely
to the way teachers call on students in class. It has struck our
observers that teachers who impress them as being aloof from the
children frequently will not use the children's names in calling on
them, but, rather, use some impersonal device such as those
listed in the outline under V : 19. Nevertheless, this is far from
being an established correlation : some teachers who appear to be
bitterly hostile to their students make frequent use of their per-

sonal names, while others who seem much closer to the students use the techniques listed under V : 19. The following, from an eighth-grade class in the United States, provides an example of a hostile teacher who generally uses the children's names:

Cyril reads. He stumbles and mispronounces the word con'-tent. After three attempts he pronounces it con-tent'. Teacher says, 'Cyril, do you or don't you know what you're reading?' She emphasizes 'do you' or 'don't you' as she gives Cyril a sharp look. 'Are you making up words to suit yourself?' Cyril looks at the teacher, smiles, then lowers his head, and reads on. He comes across a sentence stating that 'Interest is our first important point,' but he reads it, 'Interest is one of our most important point.' The teacher raises her voice as she looks at Cyril directly, and says, 'Don't add words that are not there. Alright, Jerry, you read for us.' Jerry reads softly and rapidly, and the teacher says, sternly, 'Open your mouth,' As she says this she opens her own mouth in order to say each word distinctly. Jerry stumbles over the word cumulatively but pronounces it correctly. . . .

A boy reads smoothly. He has no trouble in pronouncing the word pinioned. The teacher interrupts him to ask, 'What do we mean when we say pinioned?' The boy says, 'tied down,' and the teacher asks, 'Are you sure?' The boy shrugs his shoulders and smiles as he slowly writes the word on a piece of paper in a half-disinterested manner, The teacher says, 'That's why we don't understand what we read. What's the use of copying the word and looking up the meaning later. It is now that you need the meaning, to give the story some sense.' She looks around the room and calls on Antoinette who had her head down on her open book. 'Antoinette, you tell us all about it, since you know so much; (pause) or is it that you are too tired or too old to look?'

It is to be observed that though this teacher calls the children by name, she is hostile, ridiculing, sarcastic and belittling (V : 15) and, also, that she resents an incorrect response (V : 8). She is also irritable (V : 20), discouraging (V : 13), and acts as if the child's self-image is irrelevant (V : 28). Further, it would appear that the process is painful to the children (IV : 8), and that their frequent stumbling is evidence of anxiety (IV : 28), feelings of inadequacy, (IV : 39), and machine jamming (II : 8 : (a)).

The following provides an example of a non-hostile teacher who, nevertheless, often does not use the children's names. The observations were made in a sixth-grade American classroom:

The teacher says, 'Mike, how is your eye?' and Mike replies, 'Fine today.' The teacher says to the class, 'First I'd like to talk to you about some work in vocabulary that you handed in and on which you made some mistakes.' She goes to the board and writes the words our, are and or. She now says, 'Let's have some sentences: first with "are".' She points to a girl at the front of the room, and the girl makes up a sentence, 'Are you going too?' Teacher says, 'Yes. Another.' She points to a boy, who makes up the following sentence, 'Tom and John are going to town or for a ride.' The teacher says, 'Good. I'm glad you used or in there too.' She point to a girl, who says, 'I or Jim are going to the show.' The teacher says, 'How did you say that? Which did you put first?' The child says, 'I or .. Oh! Jim or I are going to the show.' The teacher says, 'O.K., that's better. You all seem to know how to use them right today.'

We may notice here that this teacher shows solicitude for a child's sore eye (V : 4 : (a)), that she is polite (V : 6) in phrasing her requests to the students, and that she rewards correct responses (V : 34, II : 5) and seems to take pleasure in them (V : 7). To anticipate discussion a little, this teacher attempts to be 'ego-syntonic' (XI : 1 : (a))

V : 21. *Accepts approach*; V : 22. *Repels approach*
Children in American schools, especially in the lower grades, often attempt to be near the teacher. Categories V : 21 and V : 22 are meant to take account of whether or not the teacher accepts this.

V : 23. *Accepting of child's spontaneous expressions*
The following, observed also in the sixth-grade class used as an illustration under V : 18 and V : 19, illustrates the category 'Accepting of child's spontaneous expressions'. The children have been answering questions about a story they have read, and they are to be graded on the number of correct answers; the teacher is about to tell them the grading system :

'Now I'll tell you the bad news,' she says. Several of the children moan and groan, and the teacher says, 'It's not so bad. Take off 16 for each one wrong.' The children moan some more. . . . The teacher says, 'If you have one wrong your score is 84, two wrong, you have 68, etc.' (She continues with the scores.) A girl says, 'Why don't you give us two points if we get 68 so we will have above failing?' The teacher smiles and says, 'If you miss six you get zero.' A girl says, 'Ouch, that hurts. I hope no one gets that,' and the teacher says, smiling, 'I do too.'

The spontaneous expressions of the children all stem from their anxiety about the outcome of the grading, and the teacher accepts these expressions. Of course, not all spontaneous expressions stem from anxiety; some are merely opinions elicited by the lesson or observations about things in general (IV : 17, 18). In this teacher's acceptance of the spontaneous expressions of the children, there is also a manifestation of V : 26, her ability to handle their anxiety without becoming annoyed and repressive. Obviously the categories in the outline are not mutually exclusive.

V : 29. *Defends child against peers*

The category 'Defends child against peers' was developed to take account of situations in which the teacher defends a child, not so much from physical attack, but against verbal attacks, which are the major expression of internal aggression in children's classrooms in the United States (Henry, 1957a). The following example of a teacher's so defending a child is from observations made in a fifth-grade classroom. As one child after another stands up before the class and reads a little story he has written, the other children, reinforced by the teacher's critical attitude (V : 36), proceed to demolish his work with trivial, carping criticism (IV : 34). In spite of the fact that the teacher, with a mistaken notion of what critical thinking is all about, consistently fails to praise the children's work (V : 36), she does, very occasionally, defend a child against his carping critics :

Harriet says that in Mae's story of 'Custard the Lion' Mae said ' "most bravest animal" ' and that isn't very good English.' The teacher then says, 'No it isn't, but sometimes in stories for little children they say things like that. . . .' Victor reads a story called 'The Unknown Guest'. . . . The teacher asks the class, 'Are there any words that give you the mood of the story?' Barbara says, 'He could have made the sentences a little better. . . . [After a long carpingly critical discussion of Victor's story by the children] the teacher says. 'We still haven't decided about the short sentences – perhaps they make the story more spooky and mysterious.'

V : 34. *Praises and rewards realistically*;
  V : 35. *Praises and rewards indiscriminately*
The categories 'Praises and rewards realistically' and 'praises and rewards indiscriminately' must be considered in connection with V : 27, the teacher 'Acts and/or talks as if child's self-image is fragile', for the cause of indiscriminate praise in American schools is, in considerable part, fear of hurting a child's feelings. Thus, at a polar extreme from the teacher who never praises, but is only silent or critical, is the teacher who says everything is good. Such a teacher would, in a so-called art lesson, praise all the paintings as 'fine', 'beautiful', and so on. While V : 35 is related to V : 27, it is related also to VIII : 5, 'Ignorance or error of teacher', as a limiting factor in learning, for most elementary school teachers do not know how to teach art. Since they know so little about teaching art, and possibly about art, their failure to praise or criticize with discrimination is understandable. Meanwhile, children with talent might be discouraged by hearing everything praised, whether it was actually good, bad, or indifferent. Thus indiscriminate praise becomes inadvertent discouragement.

V : 42. *The inclusive plural*
'The inclusive plural' refers to a practice, widespread among teachers at all levels in the United States, of including themselves in statements and instructions meant only for their students. Thus a teacher, referring to the students' unfamiliarity with the use of quotation marks, says, 'We haven't learnt to use them yet.' It seems that the function of this 'we' is to diminish the status-gap between pupil and teacher.

 A preliminary survey of education in non-literate societies yields the impression that the following attitudes are found among teachers there as well as in American culture :

V : 4. *Dominative*
   4(a). Integrative*
   7. *Enjoys correct response*
   13. *Discouraging*
   14. *Encouraging*

* Actually V : 4 and 4a are very complex. H. H. Anderson (Anderson and Brewer, 1945, 1946; Anderson, Brewer and Reed, 1946) has made the fundamental contribution to the elucidation of this problem.

15. *Hostile, ridiculing, sarcastic, belittling*
20. *Irritable*
27. *Acts and/or talks as if child's self-image is fragile*
28. *Acts and/or talks as if a child's self-image is irrelevant*
34. *Praises and rewards realistically*
38. *Does not punish incorrect answer or poor performance*

Other attitudes enumerated under this section V may be present in non-literate societies also, but relevant information is still so scant that one must hope that future studies will be more sensitive to this field of research.

VI. ARE SOME THINGS TAUGHT TO SOME AND NOT TO OTHERS?

The question, 'Are some things taught to some people and not to others?' raises the issue of the apportionment of the contents of a culture among its members. For, if some things are, for example, taught to girls, and others to boys, it can only be because when the young people are mature men and women they will be responsible for different things in the culture. One obvious difference between men and women with respect to apportionment is in the work men and women do, and from this has arisen the classic conception of the sexual division of labour. However, not only labour but everything else in a culture is apportioned, hence the educational process provides for much more than the division of labour but everything else in a culture is apportioned, hence the social class, and other categories of persons, for each one of these carries a different part of the cultural baggage.

As a matter of fact, the concept of apportionment implies also the broad issue of the philosophical ideas that lie behind it and ultimately determine the educational process. If the pivotal problem in a culture is man's relation to God, then religious instruction will play an important role in the education of all. But if, as in the eastern European *shtetl* culture, the pathway to God is the prerogative of males (Zborowski and Herzog, 1952), then males alone will receive formal religious instruction.

All cultures have, in addition to a general conception of man's relation to the world, some ideas about the inherent nature of children, and such ideas affect education. For example, since both nineteenth-century Calvinists (Sunley, 1954, p. 159) and twentieth-century Lepchas (Gorer, 1938, p. 305) thought children were born bad, their educational processes focused on eradicating the badness. In the same way, status systems are typically buttressed by ideas, and education is shaped to fit those ideas. One of the most widespread status differentiations is between men and women. Since in the Chinese, Hebrew and Indo-European traditions men have stood for intellect and strength, and women for emotion and weakness, the cultural baggage has been apportioned accordingly, and the educational process has differed for boys and girls.

Data is abundant in the area of differential education by sex, for the sexual division of culture has, throughout human history, been one of the most obvious and dramatic aspects of apportionment. In the west, it has been a matter for controversy. The issue pivots on a central contradiction, namely, that culture has striven *both* to unite and to separate the sexes, at the same time, thus *their unity was sought through dividing them.* The line of division was at the separation of functions, and it was this line that was *also the line of unity,* for those functions were complementary. As long as men and women do different things they need each other, and this need adds to the ties of matrimony and children. A Sirionó man without a woman cannot hunt, because she makes the string for his bow (Holmberg, 1950, p. 14)!

So, though it is correct to say that men and women are taught different things because they have different things to do, the fundamental point is that they *must* have different things to do. From this stems the pressure to keep their educational areas separate.

In the ensuing paragraphs, stress will be placed on status differences as expressed in education, but it must be borne in mind that at the base of such status differences there is always a philosophy of the differences between persons, which itself is everywhere subject to the inexorable law of apportionment.

VI : 1. *Do different age groups learn different things?*
All societies have recognized that children of different ages are capable of learning different things, although they may differ in opinion with respect to the specific age at which children are capable of learning some one thing. For example, though *shtetl* children (Zborowski and Herzog, 1952, p. 89) start to learn to

read and write at the age of three, Americans think this is premature and 'pushing' the child. On the other hand, in early eighteenth-century America, 'Boys entered Boston Latin School as
young as six and a half. They often began Latin much younger,'
and three year olds were taught to read Latin as well as English
(Calhoun, 1945, vol. 1, p. 110). Williams says of China that during the Middle Kingdom boys seven years old were taught to
count and name the cardinal points.

At eight, they must be taught to wait for their superiors, and prefer
others to themselves. At ten, the boys must be sent abroad to private
tutors, and there remain day and night, studying writing and arithmetic, wearing plain apparel, learning to demean themselves in a
manner becoming their age, and acting with sincerity and purpose.
At thirteen, they must attend to music and poetry; at fifteen they
must practise archery and charioteering. At the age of twenty, they
are in due form to be admitted to the rank of manhood, and learn
additional rules of propriety, be faithful in the performance of filial
and fraternal duties, and though they possess extensive knowledge,
must not offer to teach others . . . (Williams, 1849 vol. 1423–4).

On the whole, anthropological monographs have not dealt in
detail with the ages at which children learn particular things.
Among the few authors who do discuss age differences at
some length are Raum (1940) and Ammar (1954). Ammar has
provided a thorough timetable for Egyptian children, and
though it deals with the tasks they perform rather than the tasks
they learn, it may be safely assumed, I think, that the time-gap
between doing and learning is not great. Since he has worked it
out so carefully, and since anthropology is in need of similar
tables, it may be worthwhile to present here (Table 1) his table
for children from ages three to seven (Ammar, 1954, pp. 30–31).

There is, of course, a great difference between a record of what
children are doing and a record of what they are learning, for the
record of learning involves a study of precisely how the adult
makes known his wishes and transfers his knowledge to the child,
and/or how the child learns what the adult wishes are and
absorbs the necessary knowledge. Hence Table 1 is merely a
good start.

To return to education in early eighteenth-century Boston, it
would seem that such education has to be understood as one

Table 1

Boys

No serious tasks are expected till the age of five, whereupon they are required to work as messengers fetching goods from the shop, or running errands for their parents, uncles, etc. . . . fetching and taking things from and to other homes. Children (between five and seven) are considered to be the best messengers, especially for invitations or for asking help from neighbours, and borrowing from them, being less embarrassed, less inquisitive, and only repeating faithfully what is told to them.

In the absence of older sisters he takes care of his younger brother or sister.

Towards the end of this period he goes to the field with his older siblings, or with his father, riding behind him on donkey back or balanced in one of the camel's panniers.

Helps in carrying grass to the animals, scaring birds from the field, filling waterpots from the canal; ties or unties the cow, donkey, and camel for his father or older brother.

On the whole for him this is a stage of observation without allotted specific responsibilities. As the villagers put it, this is the period for children 'to be moistened with earth'.

Girls

Care of infants is one of the girl's main tasks at all ages, and starts as early as five, when she takes her younger sibling outside for play, or attends to him while mother is doing some domestic task.

Runs errands like boys, especially for her mother or aunt, e.g. fetching fire, bringing food or other things that need to be hidden with the dangling parts of her head cloth.

Accompanies mother to the well or to the Nile with her small pot or tin, carried on her head and supported by her lifted arms.

Helps mother in bringing fuel to the oven or the fire, consisting of millet stems, tree branches, dry animal dung, etc.

Makes her own loaf with the last bit of dough which she eats after it is baked. This is a means of her initiation to domestic tasks by being 'moistened with dough', and a reminder that 'kneading and baking' are one of the most important jobs for a girl.

phase of a total emphasis on early growing up. That was a culture in which boys 'became men at sixteen, paid taxes and served in the militia' (Calhoun, 1945, vol. 1, p. 110). With respect to the *shtetl*, the emphasis on early reading and writing of Hebrew can be understood in terms of cultural survival depending on reverence for, if not knowledge of, the Hebrew classics. In general, the age at which education in a given skill begins may be seen as a function of the total organization of the culture, including ideas about children.

At this point one may generalize and say that what children are taught at a particular time in their lives is determined by the following factors: 1. what there is to learn; 2. the objective physical and intellectual maturity of the child, as well as the members of the culture are able to perceive it; 3. the attitude toward children – which, of course, may seriously modify the cultural perception of 2; and 4. the major goals of the culture – which may be 'prestige through head-hunting', 'accumulation of capital', 'maintenance of *shtetl* culture against the gentiles', 'social mobility', and so on.

VI : 2. *Do the sexes learn different things?*

While published materials lack specifically with respect to differences in education according to age, they are rich in reports of differences in education according to sex. A few examples will suffice. The first is from contemporary Egypt (Ammar, 1954, pp. 207–8):

All the Kuttabs, except the aided one, are confined to boys. Only recently have some girls begun to attend the aided Kuttab. . . . In fact, throughout the history of Moslem Egypt the keenness on teaching girls the Koran has never been so strong as in the case of boys. MacDonald mentioned, however, that there are records of learned women who had finished a Kuttab course and proceeded to a higher educational course in either al-Azhar or the College Mosques (Madrasah); but their numbers were very small in comparison.

Of England in the eighteenth century Bayne-Powell says (1939, pp. 106, 123):

The majority of the girls of the upper classes did not go to school at all. Parents considered it a waste of money to pay for an expensive education, when a governess or waiting gentlewoman could teach them at home for £20 a year all they needed to learn. It was thought, too, as Swift complained, that a 'humour of reading books, excepting

those of devotion or housewifery, is apt to turn a woman's brain.
... that all affectation of knowledge, beyond what is merely domestic,
renders them vain, conceited, and pretending', and that 'a girl will
have all the impertinence of a pedant without the knowledge'.

[Girls] were carefully taught how to enter and leave a room, how
to get into a carriage, how to hand a cup of tea.

The curtsy was an elaborate affair of many gradations, scarcely
perceptible in some cases, and in others a fine reverance to the very
ground. It was constantly performed, even children curtsied cere-
moniously to each other when they met.

In eighteenth-century Germany, it was 'particularly difficult
for women [of the aristocracy] to cultivate their minds' (Bruford,
1935, p. 65) because of the danger of putting ignorant men to
shame. (See VI : 3.)

The Dutch both in New Netherlands and in Europe seem to
have constituted in the literate world a marked exception to the
rule that women should not have an education that made demands on the intellect or trespassed on the prerogatives of men:

The women of the Dutch Netherlands in the sixteenth and seventeenth centuries were more highly educated, better protected by the
laws, and more prominent in station than any of their contempo-
raries. On the women's judgement, prudence, foresight, everything
hinged (Calhoun, 1945, vol. 1, p. 48).

Calhoun says that foreigners disapproved of the Dutch woman's
'ascendancy', and adds, 'In New Netherlands both sexes received
education and that men and women were more equal than later
under English fashion' (1915, vol. 1, p. 167). With the exception
of the Dutch settlements, early education in the United States
followed closely the widespread European pattern of confining
female education to domestic tasks, writing, and 'social skills'. In
conversation with me, Dietrich Garhardt has suggested that the
attention given to the education of upper-class Dutch women
may have been related to the important role they played in com-
merce, even including holding partnerships in mercantile esta-
blishments.

VI : 3. *Are different groups taught different things?*
The problem of class differences in education in the United
States is well known from the work of Hollingshead (1949) and of

Warner, Havighurst and Loeb (1944). These authors describe the ways in which lower-class children in small cities are excluded from educational opportunities that would put them on the 'social elevator'. Fortes, describing education in Tale society, emphasizes that the uniformity in education there is due to absence of social stratification, but also shows that, as soon as any status factor enters the society, it is taken account of by the educational process (1938, pp. 9–10). In Samoa the *taupo*, or village princess, receives an education quite different from that of other girls (Mead, 1939, part 1, pp. 78–9).

Since in Western civilization variously privileged types of instruction were unequally apportioned according to economic level and social class, it would be well to give consideration to some data on the subject. In eighteenth-century Germany (Bruford, 1935, pp. 67, 68, 71), the nobility were ignorant, and the cultivated bourgeoisie were intellectual leaders. 'Almost all [the aristocracy] considered it beneath the dignity of a nobleman to desire any genuine scholarship.' In the second half of the same century, however, the nobility began 'to follow in the footsteps of the bourgeoisie', although it was still important for their sons to learn dancing, fencing and riding, along with modern languages. The curricula in the boarding schools for sons of the nobility, therefore, were a mixture of the social arts, including cards, chess and music, along with subjects like arithmetic, history and geography, and 'perhaps some snippets of natural science, the "curiosities" of botany, anatomy, physics and chemistry'. A little ethics and law were also included, along with meat carving! Bruford ends his discussion by stating that, 'The proper study of mankind was how to please the great.'

It is clear that regularly in western civilization some class has looked with contempt on enlightenment: knowledge in all areas has had to fight to come into existence and to survive. The history of education in England (Bayne-Powell, 1939, p. 11) and Germany (Bruford, 1935) shows, also, that enlightenment by no means always flowed from the higher to the lower classes. It would appear that as the feudal system in Europe began to disintegrate, the bourgeoisie played an important role in forcing new knowledge upon a reluctant nobility and church (Pirenne, 1937, pp. 123–4). In the history of western civilization new knowledge was a threat to traditional status relationships, whether between classes or between sexes, and fear of this threat remains. For this reason a prime effort in western civilization has been to tame new knowledge and direct it in such a way that it would strengthen the traditional social structure rather than unhinge it.

From the preceding there emerges the interesting fact that the absorption of new knowledge implies a change in the existing social structure. From this generality we may now proceed to some interesting refinements.

Let any increment in knowledge be represented by k. Then, in an infinite universe, the sum of all possible k is $K = \infty$. If we assume no limit to what mankind can learn, it follows that social structures will go through an infinite number of changes, if, in the course of an infinite history, mankind absorbs all possible knowledge. Of course, man, as Spinoza has taught us, is finite, so he cannot know everything, and hence not all possible social structures will be experienced. It is also unlikely that mankind will be around forever! But, if we assume that a great deal of knowledge will yet be absorbed by cultures, it follows that we have very many social structures ahead of us.

Now k is not a simple quantitative function: it has also a quality, which derives from its consequences for social structure. Some ks are low in social-structure relevance, others high. For example, it is of little social-structure relevance if somebody discovers a new colour for a lipstick, but if someone discovers a new basis for understanding human behaviour (e.g. Freud), this has great social-structure relevance. It is clear therefore, that we must always multiply k (increment in knowledge) by some variable factor a * (which stands for 'social-structure-relevance'), and that a (adaptation) is a function of the number of h multiplied by their corresponding a Where $a < 0$, we get $a = f(ak)$. This is a *general sociological law of knowledge and social change*. It states that social change is a function of new knowledge and the social-structure-relevance of that knowledge. (We know, of course, that social structure changes for reasons

---

* Alpha will vary with every bit of knowledge, for each bit has different social structure relevance. For example, alpha will have one *value* for a new lipstick colour and a different one for a new theory of interpersonal relations. Thus the value of alpha is always purely empirical.

other than merely new knowledge. The model expresses only the relation of change to knowledge.)

Now, we know that different status groups in a society may exclude each other from knowledge to which each group considers it has proprietary rights. Traditional India is an excellent example of a society structured in this way. In an open system, however, anyone may, theoretically, know anything there is to know.

If a closed system is inundated with knowledge (i.e. k increases greatly), it will eventually fall apart, for the magnitude of the required adaptation a will destroy the old system. On the other hand, an open-class system inundated with knowledge allows scholarship and economic exploit to create new status groups to manipulate the new knowledge. Expressing these statements as hypotheses, we may say that 1. knowledge circulates among social-status groups more readily in open social-status systems than in closed social-status systems, and 2. new intellectual horizons are revealed more readily in open social-status systems than in closed social-status systems. The evolutionary, as well as the thermodynamic, implications of these hypotheses are obvious, namely, 'Nature hates closed status systems' because they are 'counter-evolutionary' in that biologic systems must absorb energy from outside the system (von Bertalanffy, 1950).

VII. DISCONTINUITIES IN THE EDUCATIONAL PROCESS
Benedict (1938) applied the concept 'discontinuity' to that type of cultural experience in which there is a sharp break between child and adult roles. In *Coming of Age in Samoa*, Mead (1928) had discussed the problem of abrupt differences between child and adult education. Both writers urged that discontinuities create conflict and tension.

In most cultures, knowledge appropriate to one sex appears to vary primarily with age (i.e. time) and hence, all things being equal, the more that people of the same sex approximate each other in age, the more equal their knowledge. There are cultures, however, where all things are not equal, but where a specific *exclusion factor* creates a massive difference between two persons of almost equal age. Such a factor might be, for example, the withholding of certain kinds of information from a boy who has not yet passed through an initiation ceremony. In such a case there might be a crucial difference in knowledge (i.e. a discontinuity) between two boys separated by a relatively small age difference. Thus once an exclusion factor is introduced into the educational process, the learning curve can take almost any course, and a discontinuity can arise even between persons adjacent in age.

The theoretical issue in discontinuity in education does not pivot on *any* items of knowledge, but on *critical* items. In the United States it is of little significance that at twelve years of age Mary does not know the history of the Balkan Wars though her mother does. But it is of critical significance that Mary does not understand menstruation though her mother does. The issue in the study of discontinuities in education, then, is to discover whether there are critical areas of knowledge from which children are deliberately excluded by adults.

Meanwhile it is necessary to take account of the fact that the exclusion factor is often inefficient in operation, so that critical items do get to the child either in whole or in part, or in a distorted form. Though Benedict says that adults in our culture *view* the child as 'sexless', the *child* is not sexless; and he manages to find out a great deal about sex, and engage in sexual experimentation, in spite of adults. This leads to the interesting conclusion that knowledge drags role-performance after it. In less vivid language, a person possessing knowledge will tend to put it to use even in the face of social sanctions against such behaviour. This might be called 'the law of the forbidden fruit', i.e. forbidden knowledge will be put to use when the resultant rewards exceed the punishments, or when the culprit feels he can evade the consequences of breaking the law.

When the exclusion factor affects whole groups of adults, we get differentiation in the social structure. It would appear, therefore, that the exclusion factor has social structure-relevance. We infer from this that the persistence of exclusion must have as its function the prevention of social change. Armed with this inference, we may return now to the world of the child, to inquire whether the exclusion of children from certain areas of knowledge is not for the purpose of preventing social change. It seems likely, for example, that keeping knowledge of sexuality from children in American culture has served to maintain the old authoritarian family structure in which the children remained unmarried until they fought their way to independence. Among the Chagga, ignorance on the part of young women that men really do defecate is related to male prestige. Among the Hopi, keeping children in ignorance of the fact that the *kachina* dancers are men, not gods, helps maintain the moral sanction system.

When a child is excluded from knowing *all* about something of which he knows part, he tends to imagine the rest, provided he is interested. Since adults tends to fill the gap in the child's knowledge with stories, in lieu of the truth, it often becomes difficult to tell what the child has spontaneously imagined and what he has been told in stories by adults. There is this danger inherent in educational systems containing discontinuities, that they foster distorting fantasies in children, and oblige adults to lie or to maintain a silence that perplexes the child and breeds distrust. The Manus, in the Admiralty Islands, seem to constitute an exception to this, for, Mead tells us (1939, part 2), the children contemptuously thrust the adult world from them.

Today the nursery tales that formerly were told to children to explain the world they did not know have given way to television programmes which pour *their* tales into the minds of children. That is to say, young children, knowing little about what adult jobs really are, fill their fantasy world with mass-produced distortions. The following examples from interviews with nursery-school children illustrate the point. The interviews were carried out by Mrs William Gomberg.

FRANKIE: He wants to be like the Lone Ranger* when he grows up, or like any cowboy. Cowboys are all good and their only occupation is to kill bad guys, ride horseback 'real good' and fire a gun very well.
ROBSON: I don't like the Indians, they are naughty, they go where they are not supposed to. . . . I like the Lone Ranger, he shoots some cowboys: some cowboys aren't good. [Why?] Cause they were bad: they were riding and they were dead, and then they were bleeding, and that means you are dead, and when you're dead that means you are bad and you then fall down. Death is bad; you bleed and bleeding is bad. . . . He would like to be big like Lone Ranger and shoot the bad people.
NETTI: Superman* didn't come, he was far away in Brazil where I

was a baby. He's real. . . . He and Mighty Mouse,* they're real. Oh
yes; he's not make-believe. I know. I got a picture of him and he
loves me and he kisses me and he gives me things, like a sewing
machine and beer and candy and toys. Oh yes, he came to my house
and brought it to me, I saw him. No, not on TV. I see him on TV,
but this was different; he came to my house and kissed me.

ROGER: I see Lone Ranger on TV sometimes. I like him and cowboys but they shoot people and then people have to go to the hospital.
They are always mad at people cause they always shoot and they
don't like each other and that's why they shoot. People shoot but
they shouldn't do that, it's wrong to shoot one another. I don't like
to watch anything else. I ask my mother all the time, why do they
have to shoot one another and she tells me they get very mad. I don't
know if they are good people or bad people. They must be bad people
if they have to shoot one another, don't you think so? My mother
thinks so too.

MICHAEL: [He says of the programme *Calling all Cars*:] That's
the police car calling. That means to come out and fight the bad
guys. Police are good guys and they have to fight the bad people.
[He seemed disgusted at my lack of knowledge, and threw his
hands out, saying, 'Don't you know nothing?']

While in cultures characterized by unity of the social sphere
(Fortes, 1938) the play aspects of socialization tend to relate
directly to the realities of future adult roles, in American society
they become deeply enmeshed in mass-produced fantasies. The
above interviews are responses by children who act out in their
play the characters they mention in their interviews. Thus there
enters into the children's play, not the make-believe or practice
dimensions of a genuine adult world, but commercial distortions
of the world based on *adult* fantasies. The point is that the children's play becomes saturated with their *own* fantasy versions of
adult fantasies, thus 'compounding a felony'. The groundwork
for this is laid by the discontinuity in education.

* The Lone Ranger, Superman and Mighty Mouse are characters in
television shows. The Lone Ranger appears in cowboy pictures. He wears a
mask, rides a wonderful horse called 'Silver', is accompanied by a faithful
Indian companion, and always does good, defeating the 'bad guys', the evil
men. Superman can fly through the air, hold mountains in the palm of his
hand, and withstand most lethal weapons. In everyday life he is a news-
paper reporter, Clark Kent, but when he dons his magic clothing he becomes
Superman. Mighty Mouse is a Superman-like mouse.

Since discontinuity, true exclusion of children from adult knowledge, creates conflict and distortion, one might think that the phenomenon is rare. Yet, it is rather common the world over. Possibly one of the most 'popular' discontinuities in primitive education occurs in the realm of ceremonial, religion and magic, and such discontinuity is often broken at initiation. As we have noted above (I : 28), it would appear that the function of this discontinuity and the abrupt breaking of it is to effect reorganization and reorientation of the personality. The following is an illustration from the life of one Hopi :

I had a great surprise. They were not spirits, but human beings. I had recognized nearly every one of them and felt very unhappy because I had been told all my life that the kachinas were gods. I was especially shocked and angry when I saw my uncles, fathers and own clan brothers dancing as kachinas ... [but] my fathers and uncles showed me ancestral masks and explained that long ago the kachinas had come regularly to Oraibi and danced in the plaza. They explained that since the people had become so wicked ... the kachinas had stopped coming and sent their spirits to enter the masks on dance days ... I thought of the flogging and the initiation as a turning point in my life, and I felt ready at last to listen to my elders and live right (Simmons, 1942, pp. 84–7).

We have one similar example from the Chagga :

Before circumcision I was very much annoyed at being called *iseka* by those already circumcised and even by women. I was told that I would not be able to bear the pain, and that if I frowned or moved even my big toe even a little I would be beaten. A song would be composed about my cowardice, and my chances of being married spoiled. For these reasons I was very much afraid lest I should fail to stand the excruciating pains that make you a man. I had half a mind to shirk circumcision, but realized it was better to be mutilated than to be ridiculed and despised. At the time of the circumcision itself I was neither elated nor disappointed. My body felt as if benumbed, but presently I felt a pain the like of which I had not suffered before. At once a great joy welled up in me at having passed the test of pain without disgracing myself. This joy was increased by the congratulations of my relatives and their words of comfort and admiration. After my recovery I felt proud to be a man whom nobody dared to call 'hobbledehoy' (Raum, 1940: p. 310).

The phenomena of reorientation and reorganization accompanying the rupture of a discontinuity lead to the necessity for evaluating discontinuity in other than purely conflict terms. In view of the Hopi and Chagga evidence, it appears necessary to consider the possibility of a new dynamism's entering life through the burdens placed upon the personality by the need to overcome the shock of new knowledge.

VIII. WHAT LIMITS THE QUANTITY AND QUALITY OF INFORMATION A CHILD RECEIVES FROM A TEACHER? This section is not concerned with the question, 'What makes men blind?' – which alone would require a book to answer. Rather, it is confined to the question, 'When a teacher has before him a child to whom he must communicate a definite body of information, what limits the quantity and quality of the information the child receives from him?'

Before taking up in detail the ten categories in this section, it might be interesting to ask, 'Are there differences between American and non-literate cultures with respect to any of those categories?' For example, is it possible to say that the methods used to teach a skill in some non-literate culture, whether hunting, fishing, agriculture, dancing, or ceremonial, limit the proficiency with which that knowledge or skill is mastered (VIII : 1)? If there are differences among Tikopia men in fishing skill, are these differences due to the way the various men were taught, or to differences in the men themselves? Firth (1936) raises this question, but, on the whole, information on the subject is lacking from non-literate cultures. Information is lacking also for the categories:

VIII : 7. *Failure of teacher to correct pupil's mistakes*
     8. *Failure of teacher to indicate whether the pupil's*
       answers are right or wrong
     9. *Failure of teacher to respond to a question*
     10. *General vagueness or fumbling of the teacher*
None of the following considerations seems to affect the educational process in non-literate cultures:

VIII : 2. *Available time*
     3. *Quality of equipment*

4. *Distance from the object*

5. *Ignorance or error of teacher*

That is, there seems to be no time pressure; equipment seems to be adequate; the object of instruction – the land, the bow, the fish-net – is always available; the teachers seem always to know their subject matter. On the other hand, there seems to be a great deal of hostile stereotyping (VIII : 6): members of other villages may be witches or 'constipated', as among the Pilagá; or, more commonly, members of other tribes are considered non-human, and their customs absurd.

In American culture, by contrast, a pupil is limited in what he may learn from his teacher by the fact that the teacher often rushes through the lessons, lacks adequate equipment, teaches about things that are often remote from him and from the pupil either in space or time or both, and teaches subjects in which he himself is weak in knowledge. When we realize that categories VIII : 7–9 set still further limits on what children in American culture may learn, it becomes abundantly clear that it is more difficult for a child to learn in this culture than in non-literate cultures.

The complexity of classroom experience in contemporary American culture is such that the quotations which follow will reveal several limiting factors to be operating at the same time. The first examples are taken from a sixth-grade elementary-school class. The students are having an arithmetic lesson. The recorder was Amanda Chura.

TEACHER: Monitors, are you ready yet? [They shake their heads, no. Two children go to the teacher's desk to talk to her.]
TEACHER: Alright, girls, you have no time to waste. Now *I'm* waiting. Hurry!
[Some of the children have been working problems on the board. Gloria drops her ruler, looks at AC, puts hand to mouth, looks guilty. . . .]
I : 16 p.m.
TEACHER: Alright, monitors, collect the noonday problems. Alright, first class ready. Alright, let's take out our graphs that we worked on this morning. Alright, hurry up. You take too long on these problems. It should only take you about five minutes.
TEACHER: Now let's take out the graphs that you drew. Now when

we looked at our graphs before – what other words do you know that end in g-r-a-p-h? David?

DAVID: Telegraph.

TEACHER: Ray?

RAY: Phonograph.

TEACHER: Richard?

RICHARD: Paragraph.

TEACHER: Yes; and what about photograph? A photograph is a picture; it carries a message to our eyes. A telegraph carries a message.

[The teacher's asking for words ending in graph was accompanied by eager waving of hands by the children.]

TEACHER: Who would get a lot of use out of these graphs, Larry?

LARRY: The business bureaus.

TEACHER: That's right. The businessman could just look at a graph and he could read something from it.

The first thing to be noted here is the emphasis on shortage of time, and that it is not to be wasted. American children work almost constantly under the lash of time. The second point of interest is the teacher's ignorance. Words ending in 'graph' are given her by the students, and she suggests that the morpheme indicates 'message'. It is possible that the significance of the similarity among 'graph', 'photograph', and 'telegraph' may have been grasped by the students along with the (erroneous!) idea that they all 'mean' message. Where in his picture, however, would the wondering child fit 'phonograph', and, especially, 'paragraph'? The teacher avoids the problem by not responding to the waving hands of the children. Third, note her lack of concreteness about businessmen's use of graphs.

The lesson now turns to review of the problems of perimeters.

TEACHER: We'll do a little reviewing of measuring by feet, inches and yards. That measure is called linear – it is along a line. What could you measure by feet and inches? Roy?

ROY: A swimming pool.

TEACHER: A swimming pool? No, I don't think so . . .

TEACHER: I want you to make up six problems and work them: two with perimeter, two with square measure, and two with cubic measure. Right now we will make up a few examples.

I : 45

[David raises his hand practically right away.]

TEACHER: David?

[David starts.]

TEACHER: Wait a minute, I can't hear you. You talk too low anyway. Now stand up nice and straight.

DAVID: A farmer had a field 30 by 40 feet. He bought another of the same size. What are the dimensions of both together?

TEACHER: Now you don't mean dimensions, do you? You already gave us that.

DAVID: I mean perimeter.

TEACHER: Alright, now repeat the problem.

[David repeats.]

TEACHER: *You'll* have to tell if it's the right answer or not, I'm not in on this one.

[AC notes: The way she said it made it appear to me that she didn't understand the problem or else couldn't figure it out.

David calls on Arthur and Arthur answers 280.]

TEACHER: Yes. Now let's have another one; don't make it too hard. Make it so we can all work it in our heads. Now make up a problem for square measure. Make it easy enough. Save the hard ones for your written problems.

Obviously there are three possible solutions to David's problem, depending on whether the fields are separate, contiguous on their long sides, or contiguous on their short sides, and the teacher was not able to solve it.

This was followed by another 'hard' problem, and the teacher said, 'Alright, we won't give the answer, but we'll tell how to work it right now.' The teacher then became irritated and issued a flurry of commands. At 2 : 00 p.m. the observer recorded: 'Teacher still sits there staring at them with that mean look. The sudden burst of irritation suggests that she was upset by the problems.'

At this point it is useful to remark on some limiting factors that are not listed in the outline but are apparent in the above examples. It has been noted that the teacher introduced into the discussion of graphing a consideration of the meaning of the morpheme 'graph'. In so doing, she distracted the children from the immediate subject matter. We might call this an instance of irrelevant introduction of polyphasic learning (Henry, 1955a). It might not have been so bad if the teacher had given an adequate explanation of the meaning of the morpheme, but, instead, she merely generated confusion about it. Thus, the irrelevance interfered with learning in two ways: it interrupted the learning of graphs, and was itself erroneous.

The teacher's command to David to stand up straight while he was reciting belongs in this same general category of irrelevant introduction of polyphasic learning. Of what importance to arithmetic is it that David stand up straight while he presents his problem?

A second limiting factor is listed in the outline as V : 5, insecurity of teacher. In the above example, the teacher's insecurity further muddied the waters of knowledge.

We turn now to a classroom in which, according to the system used in some American cities, bright students are taught together with slow students who are a year ahead of the bright ones in grade. The lesson is on geography, the recorder is Ella Brown, the teacher is a man, and the students are a combination of the grades sixth-high and seventh-low. As in the example above, the children are very eager.

TEACHER: Look at page 206. Where would you find Portugal?
[Several children gave the boundaries of Portugal and the countries that lie nearest to it. All the children were talking at once.]
TEACHER: Now find Switzerland. Where is Switzerland, Essie?
ESSIE: Kind of north of Italy.
TEACHER: Alright. Now where is Denmark?
GIRL: Sticking out into the North Sea.
TEACHER: Genevieve Wells. What is Denmark that Switzerland and Portugal are not?
GENEVIEVE: A seaport.
TEACHER: Oh, no! (Disappointedly) Lisbon is one of the largest seaports in the world.
CHILDREN: It's a peninsula.
TEACHER: That's right. What is a peninsula? [He calls on several children who do not give the right answer. Then he calls on Bob, Susan, Phillip. Melvin's hand is waving among others. Teacher calls on him.]
MELVIN: A peninsula is a piece of land surrounded on three sides by water.
TEACHER (very enthusiastically): Yes, that's right; a peninsula! A peninsula is a piece of land surrounded on three sides by water.

What do these three countries [Portugal, Switzerland, Denmark] have in common?
[Linda and Melvin have their hands up.]
TEACHER: Linda.
LINDA: They're small.
TEACHER: Yes, they're all small. Now look at the picture on page 215. What are the women doing? The children look at the picture and a girl answers that they are drawing water.
TEACHER: Yes. In many of these countries there is no plumbing. Why do you think they have no plumbing? Several hands are up.
[Teacher calls on Essie.]
ESSIE: It's too expensive.
TEACHER: Yes, it's too expensive.
[Linda's hand is up. Teacher calls on her by name.]
LINDA: It's a backward country.
TEACHER: Yes, it's a backward country.
[The picture shows a number of women with earthenware vessels drawing water from a well that seems to be in a central place.]

Let us discuss in order the points raised by this lesson.

1. The teacher, by failing to adequately correct Genevieve (VIII: 7), permits her and the rest of the students to remain confused about the difference between a port and a country. 2. Considering the distance of these children from Europe (VIII: 4) and their general provincialness, it is important to correct such a misconception, even though it might seem on the surface that the misconception is merely inadvertent. 3. Generation upon generation of American children have been enthusiastically taught by teachers that a peninsula is a body of land surrounded on three sides by water. One wonders: (a) what is the reason for the enthusiasm over *this* relatively unimportant fact, and (b) of what importance is it to know what a peninsula is? Emphasis on one relatively insignificant item such as this tends to make it stand out, and exercises a limiting effect on the learning of more important data. This plays a role in narrowing the perceptual field. 4. Since Portugal, Denmark and Switzerland are grouped together as small, the child's conception of them becomes stereotypic (VIII: 6), thus obscuring the great differences among them. This kind of teaching lays the groundwork for a stereotyped world divided into large (important, significant, prestigeful)

countries, and small (insignificant) ones. 5. Portugal, Switzerland and Denmark are grouped together as backward and lacking plumbing. Here we deal not only with stereotyping but also with ignorance on the part of the teacher (VIII : 5). All these elements of a learning situation have profound influence on the child's conception of the rest of the world, even to influencing his later voting behaviour and his attitude toward war and peace. Further, we must remember that this teacher probably thinks and believes as he is teaching the children to think and believe, and that *he* votes and has ideas on the 'international situation' too!

These teaching failures, considered together, are related to the following features of American culture. 1. The vast size of the available body of knowledge. 2. The absence of the teacher's role-performance of the specific knowledge he is required to impart. 3. The low status of teachers. 4. The remoteness of the consequences of teaching failure. 5. The orientation of the total system. 6. The obsolescence of knowledge.

1. In societies inundated with knowledge, like contemporary industrial societies, we encounter such enormous differences in knowledge among individuals that many may be unaware of even the existence of whole bodies of knowledge. This is absolutely different from non-literate cultures, where, although some people may not know some of the things there are to know, everyone knows what knowledge exists. As knowledge increases in any *culture*, ignorance tends to increase in *individuals*, for these come to know less and less of the total available information. The quip that, 'A college professor is a person who knows less and less about more and more', applies to everyone in contemporary culture, and especially to schoolteachers since they are expected to teach many subjects.

2. In section VII, on discontinuities, it was stated that knowledge drags role-performance after it. It would follow that, in the *absence* of role-performance, there is no knowledge: a man who has never taught would, ordinarily, not know how to teach (although he might know something about teaching). This same reasoning applies to teachers who have no role-involvement in the *subject matters* they teach. That is, they cannot be said to really have knowledge of those subject matters. For example,

anthropologists would not ordinarily tend to make mistakes about the geography of areas on which they specialize, for their role-performance enforces knowledge of those areas; but elementary-school teachers who have never been to Europe, or worked in a travel agency or an importing or exporting company, might have but the haziest notions of the geography of Europe. A draftsman or a surveyor would be expected to be able to calculate a periphery rapidly and correctly, for his role-performance requires this. But a teacher is role-involved only in teaching; he knows about peripheries only at second hand, and therefore is not unlikely to make mistakes in calculating them. In stark contrast with contemporary industrial societies, teachers in all non-literate cultures are role-involved in what they teach: archery is taught to the children by accomplished hunters, agriculture by husbandmen, religion by men and women who practise what they preach (whether it be good or evil!), and so on.

3. Since most elementary-school teachers teach the same limited number of subjects year in and year out, one might conjecture that they ought to know those subjects very well. But this cannot be expected unless they are given satisfying incentives in money or prestige. Since they are given neither incentive in American culture, teachers tend to stay at the lowest level of performance that is acceptable to their administrations.

4. In non-literate cultures, the consequences of an adult's failure to properly teach culturally requisite skills would be immediately felt. For example, the boy who was inadequately taught to hunt would be an unsuccessful hunter, with the result that both he and his kin-group teacher would suffer hunger. In contemporary American culture, the involvement of the teacher with his students is more remote. There are probably teachers who do experience student failure in terms of concern about the student's life-chances, but, for the most part, American culture does not encourage such concern, and it certainly does not make the teacher suffer so directly for want of it. A teacher's standing may depend in some degree on his pupil's achievements, but this does not imply personal involvement in his students' *welfare*, and the lack of deep involvement permits him to remain at a minimal level of efficiency. Firth's remarks on education in Tikopia (1936,

p. 148) underscore the relationship between personal involvement and expertness in teaching, and also bring out a further fact, the importance to the teacher of his student's gratitude:

The training of a boy ... is often due to the interest of one of his mother's brothers in him. If this man is an expert in any branch of knowledge he will probably see to it that his nephew receives some of the results of his experience. If he is a noted canoe-voyager and fisherman he will pass on his store of information in the finer points of his craft to the lad: especially will he show him the location of fishing-banks, a prized set of data not possessed by all fishermen. In dirges composed to the memory of mother's brothers reference is not infrequently made to this sort of assistance. A grandfather may take a great interest in a child's upbringing and may provide him with traditional lore, names of family ancestors and their history, tales of ancient fights and immigrations. ... The transmission of details of family ritual and more esoteric information concerning the family religious life is essentially the role of the father, and not infrequently does the head of the house lament the fact of his own comparative ignorance due to his father's early death.

5. The orientation of the total educational system is an important factor at the root of teaching failure. For example, in the United States there is a sharp division between those who think that the primary function of a teacher is to facilitate a child's emotional adjustment, and those who think that the teacher's main function is to teach subject matter. In non-literate societies, education does not face this problem. While it is obvious that this and similar dilemmas arise because man is groping toward a new adaptation, it is also clear that they are related to the complicated role-involvement of the American teacher. That is, constantly teaching subject matters of which his knowledge is imperfect, he reaches, in his anguish, toward a subject matter in which he can imagine himself to have some broad competence. Alas, it is only too clear that he does not even have expertise in 'adjustment' (Henry, 1955a, 1957b)!

6. The dictionary definition of *obsolete* is 'gone out of use'. In this sense, almost no knowledge becomes obsolete in a literate culture with an interest in history: knowledge of alchemy and of the building of pyramids and battering rams still has a use in the history of science. Whether for historical or other reasons, it is

difficult to disuse knowledge in a culture with written records. Nevertheless, there is a sense in which knowledge does go out of use even in a literate culture: it becomes obsolescent if there is no role attached to it.

Since the next examples I give are derived from elementary-school classes in ancient history, I shall discuss the obsolescence of knowledge, and its relation to social role, in the context of ancient and nearly forgotten things. Nowadays, there are still people who know the ancient art of throwing the discus and can teach it, but, since we no longer hold the polytheistic beliefs of the ancient world from which the art comes, there are no priestesses of Athena among us, and the knowledge of how to be a priestess to Athena is dead. What little remains of the knowledge associated with the roles of priestess and oracle is well known only to ancient historians, i.e. to persons who specialize in knowledge of archaic roles and the associated knowledge. Parenthetically, the fact that little of the technical knowledge that went along with these roles is available today testifies to the validity of the generalization that knowledge and role are indissolubly linked.

Let us now pictures the sixth-grade teacher who is supposed to teach the history of ancient Greece. She suffers from all the five disabilities listed above, she has never been to Europe, and, above and beyond these, she is obliged to teach about a civilization most of the roles of which have disappeared. Let us look at excerpts from the record of the performance of such a teacher and her pupils. The observations were made by Amanda Chura:

TEACHER: We've been reading about this parade in Greece to honour Athena. Why did they honour her?
PAT: She gave wisdom.
TEACHER: What else?
NORMA: I think she symbolized something.
TEACHER: The Greeks had beliefs. What do we call them today?
CHILD: Myths.
TEACHER: And these are read by children today. What Greek building have we read about? I should say temple.
CHILD: Parthenon.

[The teacher now talks about carved stone with animals or figures and these are raised.]

TEACHER: What do we call this?

CHILD: Bal-relief.

TEACHER: It looks like bas but it's really bal-.

TEACHER: The Oracle of Delphi represented Apollo. There was a woman there to answer questions, but Apollo was not a woman. Today people go to places where they make you believe that the dead speak. I don't know how real this oracle was.

TEACHER: Let's look at the map. It is in the book. I see a lot of people haven't even bothered to turn the page. Come on now.

[Teacher names Olympia and other places.]

TEACHER: Start reading Sharon.

[Darius is not paying a bit attention, but is looking to the back of the room. Antoinette is talking to her neighbour.

Teacher explains what is meant by foreign birth. If a male is not born in Greece but in a foreign country he is not eligible to compete in the Olympic games. ... Somebody says that the Olympic Festival is like the Muny Opera (i.e. the St Louis Municipal Summer Opera where musical comedies like *Oklahoma* and *Guys and Dolls* are performed).]

TEACHER: Well, yes, but just a little.

TEACHER: What great difference was there between the purposes of Athens and Sparta, Pat?

PAT: Athens was a city of beauty and Sparta a city of war.

TEACHER: I agree with the Athens part but not with Sparta, David?

DAVID: Spartans were trained to be soldiers while Athenians were interested in their city.

TEACHER: Yes, a good answer. [She repeats it.] We can go to college and take subjects just about art and music. Of course we have to take English and Language, but we can major in art. Why have the stories of the battles of Marathon and Thermopylae been told through the ages?

CHILD: Because they fought so bravely.

TEACHER: Yes, because they fought so bravely. In our country we have a similar example in Remember the Alamo. [In 1836 a group of Texans, defending the fortress Alamo against Mexican troops, was destroyed. For many years the cry 'Remember the Alamo' was the rallying cry of those Texans who fought against Mexico for independence.]

Since the teacher is dealing with a social system the roles of

which have disappeared, she attempts to make the subject matter
live by using bad analogies from contemporary roles: the Oracle
at Delphi is likened to a vague 'place where they make you believe
that the dead speak', and the Olympic competition is compared
by teacher and a student to a musical-comedy performance. Since
all ancient Athenians and Spartans have disappeared, the teacher
and students accept the empty cliché that 'Spartans were trained
to be soldiers while Athenians were interested in their city.' Thus
the fact that the knowledge about ancient Greece has become
obsolescent, in the sense intended here, leads teacher and students
into ignorance. Further revealed in the excerpts is the guided
recall (II:7) method of instruction, according to which students
are required to remember separate 'facts' but receive no integrated
picture of ancient Hellenic life and thought. This, too, is a limitation on learning, and, in this connection, it is relevant to note
the instances of inattention by students (Darius and Atoinette).

IX. WHAT KINDS OF CONDUCT CONTROL (DISCIPLINE)
     ARE USED?

In this section I distinguish between order and discipline. 'Order'
is defined here as a state in which a person is oriented toward
social goals, while 'discipline', in the sense intended here, refers
to methods used to prevent disruptive behaviour. An orderly
person is essentially a thinking person highly motivated toward
social goals; while, in the present context, a disciplined individual
is one who is merely controlled in his outward conduct. Discipline *can* work in the service of order, and often does, but not
always. For example, a child sitting quietly in his seat in class
may detest the work. Thus he is outwardly disciplined but is, in
the present definition, disorderly, for he is not oriented toward
the social goal, i.e. the lesson. On the other hand, a child oriented
toward social goals could not be undisciplined, because disruptive behaviour is generally antithetical to social goals.

Order and discipline, or, rather, order versus descipline, is an
ancient issue in western culture. In the winter of 431 B.C., in the
course of delivering the panegyric at a public funeral for war
casualties, the Athenian Pericles compared the Lacedaemonians
with the Athenians as follows:

In education, again, we leave it to our opponents to cultivate manliness by a laborious training from their tender years upwards, while we, with our undisciplined life, are as ready as they to face every reasonable danger. . . . the fact that we preserve a military spirit by a life of ease instead of deliberate hardship and by a natural rather than an artificial courage gives us a double advantage. We are not compelled to anticipate the rigours of war, yet we face them, when they come, as courageously as those who are in perpetual training (Toynbee, 1953, p. 39, quoting Thucydides).

This was the attitude of men who lived by laws 'whose moral sanction is so strong that there is no need for them to be written' (Toynbee, 1953, p. 39, quoting Thucydides).

Pericles's speech shows that the issue of order versus discipline was joined more than 2000 years ago. It is still with us today. Something of this nature must have been in the minds of the Russian educators, P. Yesipov and N. K. Goncharov, when they formulated the following (Counts and Lodge, 1947, pp. 94, 96, 97):

A state of discipline cannot bear merely an outer character. The education of children in conscious discipline. Without discipline and habits of organization one cannot study, one cannot work. But it is not merely a question of ensuring the *discipline* of pupils during the school years. Before the teacher stands a much deeper task: the cultivation in children of a *state of discipline* as a high quality of communist morality and one of the most important traits of character. The development of this quality in children is linked with the task of preparing future citizens of the Soviet state who will act from a sense of public duty and will possess a feeling of responsibility before the socialist Motherland. . . .

A state of discipline cannot bear merely an outer character. The qualities [of discipline] require an inner condition. Conscious discipline cannot rest on a foundation of fear. . . . It is important that our pupils desire and strive to become disciplined, not because of external pressure but because of their own voluntary promptings. It is important that their own active disciplinary powers function and that they have an inner harmony with discipline and a desire to achieve it. Such discipline leads inevitably to self-discipline. . . .

The basic conditions for the cultivation of conscious and firm discipline in pupils are clearly outlined in a recent decree of the People's Commissariat of Education of the RSFSR: 'The discipline of pupils is nurtured by the general practice and the whole content of the work of the school: skilful teaching of school subjects, strict regimen for the entire school life, unwavering observation by each pupil of the 'Rules for School Children', firm organization of the children's collective, and rational use of measures of rewards and punishments. The leading role in this work belongs to the teacher.'

In the thinking of Pericles and the Russian educators, it would appear, discipline is an ideal inner state, a moral principle, a trait of character. This is what is meant here by 'order'.

When we turn now to the more specific problems of education, we discover that the need to exercise conduct controls over the child during instruction in formal skills arises almost exclusively in literate cultures, and it is the difficulties arising in connection with this need that are the concern of the present section.

Since school children of all ages in the United States tend to be unruly, much of a teacher's energy goes into the effort to maintain conduct controls, for an undisciplined class cannot learn a subject matter, i.e. it is oriented away from the social goals by its disruptive behaviour. Thus an undisciplined class falls naturally into disorder. The ability to maintain discipline in a classroom seems to consist of the following components: 1. the specific techniques available to the teacher for the purpose; 2. the attitudes of the teacher (V); 3. the characteristics of the students (covered in part in section IV); and 4. the teacher's manipulation of the instruction itself (much of this is included in section II, but some is found in section V also). To these we might add 5. the attitude of the culture toward knowledge; and 6. the nature of the cultural ideals. These, however, would affect order largely through the person of the teacher in interaction with the students.

In the extracts from observations of American classrooms we will see that the techniques employed to exert conduct control are rarely used with a moral implication, or with the implication by the teacher that some deeply felt social ideal is being violated. Rather, the reason the student is commanded, threatened, or reprimanded in connection with walking around, talking to his neighbour, or daydreaming, is simply because it interferes with work, or because it offends the teacher. From studying disciplinary mechanisms year after year in American classrooms, one derives the pervasive impression that discipline has become detached from a socially significant moral base.

In the outline, twenty techniques for maintaining discipline have been listed. A finer coding might discriminate further, and separate listing of all the idiosyncratic devices grouped under 19, 'Special stratagems', would expand the list even more. The list as it stands, however, is adequate for the present purpose of illustrating techniques used for conduct control in one contemporary industrialized culture, the United States.

Not all American teachers use the same techniques, and even widely-used techniques, like 8 ('command') and 5 ('reprimand'), are employed more frequently by some teachers than by others. Furthermore, teachers using 8 and 5 may use them in qualitatively different ways: some teachers may be sarcastic in their reprimands, and some may be gentler than others in issuing commands. Always it must be borne in mind that the image of a teacher as a disciplinarian is tempered by other things – especially by V ('What is his attitude?'). For example, a strict disciplinarian might also joke with his students and permit them to argue or joke with him. Thus, study of IX alone, and study of IX in association with V, IV ('What is the attitude of the student?'), and II ('What are the teaching methods?') suggest a great variety of discipline-maintaining patterns, each peculiar to different types of teachers and to different types of students: first graders as compared with fourth graders, high-school students as compared with elementary-school students; incipient delinquents as compared with more conforming children, and so on.

Illustration of the categories in this section on discipline requires considerable fragmentation of the data, thus each category that is discussed will be listed according to the number it bears in the outline, and each illustration will be followed by the code letter of the observer and the year of the observation. Protocols have been selected only for the years 1957, 1958 and 1959.

IX : 3. *Sense of propriety*
The children in this fifth-grade class are about to be the audience for another class which is going to show off the Easter bonnets they

have made. The teacher says to her children : if we're going to be an audience we have to be very, very polite. Just admire them.

This observation also embodies IX : 10 (*'We' technique*) and IX : 15 ('Putting the child on his mettle').

TEACHER: Wait a minute, Gertie; someone is very rude behind you – someone very nice too.

This observation also embodies IX : 11 (*Instilling guilt*) and IX : 12 (*Cessation of activity*).

The students are seventh and eighth graders. The teacher had to step out of the room for a moment and it became a bit noisy. When the teacher returned he said : in a calm, soft, conversational tone to the very still class, I am disappointed at some people's manners. I am talking to someone out here in the hall and you people are talking and mumbling and having fun when there is plenty of work to do.

This observation also embodies IX : 11 (*Instilling guilt*).

In this first grade class the children are having a reading lesson. The word *sailboat* has come up, some children have failed to identify it in the reader, others are eagerly waving their hands, and some in the front seats are leaning forward and shaking their hands for attention. The teacher, in an annoyed voice, says, How would you like it if I did that to you?

This observation also embodies IX : 5 : d (*Impersonal reprimand*) and IX : 11 (*Instilling guilt*).

It will be noted that, if any morality is at issue in these observations, it is the morality of decorum. The third observation seems to imply that disorder both violates decorum and also interferes with work.

IX : 4. *Affectivity*

The category 'Affectivity' has been explored at length by Henry (1959). The essential point is that the teacher attempts to keep the children under control by making himself a love object to them, and awakening in them both a fear of loss of love should they do anything to offend him, and a sense of guilt when they have offended him. One example, taken from a reading lesson in Mrs Thorndyke's third-grade class (the children are about 8–9 years old), will illustrate this point. The observer is Henry. On this day, the children are asking each other questions about the story, instead of being asked questions by the teacher. There are twenty-five children in the class, but the group to be described is made up of the dozen or so best readers, who sit facing each other on two rows of chairs in the front of the room. At 10:27 a.m. Mrs Thorndyke is standing behind one of the rows:

She pats Alfred to restrain him and he shows a slight tendency to withdraw. There is a loud burst of noise. Mrs. Thorndyke's hand is on Alfred and he seems to wish to get out. Now her hand is on Arty, who makes no move. Teacher pats and strokes Matty who also makes no move to withdraw. Now Teacher is standing behind Arty, lightly passing her finger-tips over his neck. She goes back to Arty, puts a hand on Alfred to restrain him. He makes withdrawal signs. Alfred and Arty are now interlocking *their* hands in the air and Alfred is talking to Arty. 10:32 Teacher stops behind Otto to restrain him. Her hands are on his cheeks; his tongue goes in the direction of his right cheek and pushes it out as he closes his eyes. When Mrs Thorndyke withdraws her hands, his eyes pop open as if he had suddenly awakened. Mary, who previously was holding onto Mrs Thorndyke as the teacher stroked the child's arm, has now slumped in her seat. Teacher goes to her, puts her arms around her and pulls her back. Mary takes Teacher's hand. Alfred is talking and Mrs Thorndyke pats and strokes him. He does not withdraw this time. Alfred is now talking to Arty and Teacher is stroking Alfred. Again he does not withdraw. Now Alfred caresses Otto and Arty caresses Alfred. 10:38 Malcolm asks questions now and all the children say his questions have been asked. Mrs Thorndyke says, 'My only objection to that question is that it can be answered by either yes or no.' She strokes Matty. All this time the questions are being asked and there is great excitement among the children. Sherry asks questions and Teacher says, 'We've gone over that.' She strokes Matty and he does not resist. She touches Mary flutteringly with her finger tips.

Now Mrs Thorndyke terminates the lesson, and the papers with the questions are collected. Suddenly she becomes very grave and silent. She later told me that Mary had answered a snippity 'no' to something Teacher had said. Now Mrs Thorndyke says, '*My, I'm terribly disappointed.*' There is absolute silence, and Mrs Thorndyke says, 'Matty, you're excused to go to your seat.' She later told me it was because he's a general all-round talker and wouldn't quiet down. Matty goes to his seat looking very unhappy, his lips compressed. The room is silent now.

Now Group 2, the poorer readers, occupies the seats deserted by Group 1. Teacher seems very tired now, and goes through the lesson mechanically. Her voice is weak and she leans against the blackboard. Time, approximately 10:50.

IX:9. *Command question or request*
'Let's sit down please.' This example also illustrates **IX:10** (*'We' technique*), for the teacher uses the first person plural although the command-request is intended for the pupils only.

IX:12. *Cessation of activity*

Teacher says, Bill and Joe, would you like to leave the room? She is silent for a long time.

This example also embodies **IX:14** (*Threat*).

There is an increase in noise and teacher says, Just a moment, Mary. Teacher looks briefly at two boys who are talking, and then back at Mary. Begin again, Mary.

This example also embodies **IX:16** (*Non-verbal signal*), for a look is a non-verbal signal.

Teacher says, Wait, we can't hear because someone is talking. Several children had been talking but they quieted when she spoke.

The children are noisy again. Teacher says, Wait a minute. I don't want any more noise or moving around in the room. We'll wait until everything is quiet. This is a school and everything is going to be quiet.

This example also embodies **IX:5:d** (*Impersonal reprimand*), **IX:8** (*Command*), and **IX:10** (*'We' technique*).

IX:13. *Group sanction*
The following example is from a class of fourteen-year-old unruly delinquent and near-delinquent children:

[The students are rehearsing a play. The teacher, Sa, is his own recorder. The record reads:] I notice Herb goofing* around while waiting for his cue, and I say 'Hold it, everyone, Herb is putting on his own little show. Let's take time out to watch him.' Herb says, 'Aw, I'm not doin' nuttin'.' Ben says, 'Yeah, he goofs around all the time until it's time to act and then who clams up† and acts stupid?' Bob (the class bully) says, 'Let's get him.' Bob goes to attack Herb, and the teacher says, 'Bob, we don't need that stuff. Herb will straighten up, won't you, Herb?' Herb says, 'Aw, I ain't bothering nobody I know my part.'

This example also embodies IX:24 (*Encourages peer-group control*).

Some teachers have been observed to encourage peer-group control in a more systematic and open way. When a child does something of which such a teacher disapproves, he may call upon the other students to 'try' the culprit and punish him (Henry, 1957a; 1959).

IX:15. *Putting the child on his mettle*
To put a person 'on his mettle' is to convey to him that the situation he faces is a challenge. When a teacher, in order to keep his pupils quiet, says, 'You are on your honour' he is simply telling them that their ability to maintain discipline is a challenge to their 'honour'.

IX:19. *Special stratagems*
Some teachers develop purely idiosyncratic stratagems for maintaining discipline, but these stratagems are interesting because any one of them might some day become relatively institutionalized. For example, the use of affectivity, excessive politeness and turning the maintenance of discipline over to the students, now characteristic of some suburban schoolteachers in the United States (Henry, 1959), are relatively new developments in disciplinary techniques for grammar-school children, but will probably become more generalized in American culture in the future.

*To *goof* is to fail or do nothing. 'I goofed off' means 'I did nothing when I was supposed to be busy'. 'I goofed' means 'I failed' or 'I made a mistake'.
† To *clam up* means to become silent, i.e. to shut tight like a clam.

IX : 21. *Using a higher power*
Sometimes responsibility for discipline is shifted by the person who is disciplining the child to some higher authority, human or non-human. In the latter event, it might be a god or goblin who, it is claimed, will punish the child for misbehaviour. In American schools, the higher power is generally the (very human) principal or vice-principal. Thus :

The teacher looks at the class disapprovingly, pauses, and says, 'Just a minute. This girl right here. Leave now. The best place for you is the principal's office.' The girl leaves the room.

IX : 22. *Exclusion*
'Exclusion' is most commonly effected by sending the misbehaving child out of the room temporarily. Of course, this is also IX : 23 (*Punishment*). An occasional teacher develops an idio-syncratic form of exclusion, such as the following :

Teacher looks up and catches Katy over by her neighbour. Teacher says, 'Will you come over here please,' and she points to the floor on the left side of her desk. Katy comes over and sits down on the floor next to the teacher's desk.

Again, this is IX : 23. But the incident is coded also as IX : 22 because Katy is subjected to a kind of exclusion in being separated from the rest of the class.

The multiplicity of techniques used by teachers to maintain discipline in American schools is related to the severity of the disciplinary problem; the severity of the disciplinary problem is related to the fact that the children are not interested in being educated; the children are not interested in being educated because of the lack of unity between education and the rest of the social sphere. It may also be that the children lack interest because the social goals are uninspiring even when they can be clearly perceived – and who can clearly perceive them? In that case there would be little impetus to that kind of order of which Pericles spoke in his panegyric, and hence the children would fall into disorder, which is the root of the problem of discipline.

X. WHAT IS THE RELATION BETWEEN THE INTENT AND THE RESULTS OF EDUCATION?*

Implied in the teacher-pupil relationship is that the teacher teaches something, let us say science, and that the pupil learns it. However, the teacher not only gives instruction in a subject matter but also does many other things – like being sweet or sarcastic, telling the child to stand up straight and take his hands out of his pockets, or giving a pat on the back. Thus the child may not only 'learn science', but at the same time also learn to hate the sarcastic teacher or to love the benign one, to loathe standing up straight, to enjoy being patted on the back, etc., etc. A general theory of unintended learning should take account of this variety of things the teacher does as he teaches. At the same time it should try to include also his intent or purpose. Since, as the teacher practices his art, he has an intention, all teaching activity is a logical product of these intentions and what the teacher actually does. This formulation seems general enough to cover all cases of social learning. We may note in passing that all intentions are capable of translation into action – though some of them may never be so translated.

It is rarely true that a teacher has only one intention. Nowadays, most American elementary-school teachers seem to have a variety of them: they not only want to teach subject matter, but in addition they may want their students to be good citizens, to work hard, to live comfortably, to love their parents and the teacher, to be orderly, to have spiritual values, and so on. Accordingly, such teachers express this variety of intentions in a great variety of behaviours, which may or may not be logically related to their subject matter. We cannot predict the total consequences of this on a relatively responsive and plastic child. Even after the most careful observation and analysis of all of a teacher's actions and inferred intentions, much of what is learned by the pupil in the classroom remains, by and large, indeterminate. This fact need not, however, deter us from the attempt to study it. Of course, the more a teacher is trained to limit his intentions and his actions, the greater is the predictability of the consequences of his teaching.

*Previous publications on this problem are: Henry, 1955a; 1955b; 1957a; 1957b; Rabin, 1959; Spindler, 1959.

To this point, we have been examining classroom learning with the teacher as the centre of analytic focus. However, the pupils' potentialities for response to the teacher are central to analysis both of the relation between the intentions and actions of the teacher, on the one hand, and of what the student learns, on the other. For example, it is crucial to the understanding of a spelling competition that we be aware of the pupils' potentiality for response to a competitive situation, for, if the overwhelming majority of the children are not already competitive *children*, the spelling competition will fail. Again, we can comprehend a teacher's telling her pupils not to paint with dark colours because they indicate unhappiness, only if we assume that both teacher and students feel that unhappiness is somehow culturally unacceptable (Henry, 1955a).

Such considerations enable us to draw the conclusion that *for the actions and intentions of the teacher there are, in all cultures, complementary responses and response tendencies in the pupils.* The complementary *response* can occur only if the teacher is able to mobilize the students' latent, culturally-determined attitudes, but this he should be able to do because he is a product of the same culture as his students and should know intuitively their social character. The complementary *response* is therefore the response the teacher wants. Complementary *attitudes*, on the other hand, are latent, culturally standardized, tendencies to *give* the culturally acceptable response under the proper circumstances, e.g. a teacher's demand for the response.

Though complementarity exists when the pupil responds to the teacher as desired, e.g. he competes with his fellows when directed to do so as in a spelling competition, some children who *participate* actively might nevertheless *react* inwardly to the spelling competition *antithetically*, i.e. with anxiety and tendencies to withdraw. Thus, while it is probable that in the usual social-learning situation most of the attitudes of the children would be complementary, some could be covertly antithetical. Many might be neither complementary nor antithetical, but, rather, 'indeterminate'.

As an approximate definition of the term 'indeterminate' let us say that an indeterminate attitudinal response is one not readily predictable from knowledge of the structure of the learning situation alone. If we ask, 'Not readily predictable by whom?' the answer is (a) by the organizer of the lesson being taught; and (b) by the person who hears only a formal account of the lesson without being present at it. Indeterminate and antithetical responses as covert *meta*-responses – they *go along with* the lesson, but are features that the teacher, perhaps, would rather not have there. To illustrate, there follows material on a game of 'spelling baseball' in a fourth-grade class observed by Henry (1955a).

Children form a line along the back of the room. There is to be 'spelling baseball', and they have lined up to be chosen. There is much noise, but teacher quiets them. Teacher has selected one boy and one girl and sent them to front of room to choose their sides. As the boy and girl pick children to form their teams, each child chosen takes a seat in orderly succession around the room. Apparently they know the game well. ... Now Tom, who has not yet been chosen, tries to call attention to himself, in order to be chosen. Dick shifts his position more in direct line of vision of the choosers so that he may be chosen. Jane, Tom and Dick, and one girl whose name observer does not know, are the last to be chosen. ... Teacher now has to remind choosers that Dick and Jane have not been chosen. ... Teacher gives out words for children to spell, and they write them on the board. (Each word is a 'pitched ball', and each correctly spelled word is a 'base hit'. The children move from 'base to base' as their teammates spell the words correctly.) With some of the words the teacher gives a little phrase: 'Tongue – watch your tongue; don't let it say things that aren't kind; butcher – the butcher is a good friend to have; dozen – twelve of many things – knee – get down on your knee; pocket – keep your hands out of your pocket, and anybody else's. No talking!' Teacher says, 'Three outs,' and children say, 'Oh, oh!' ... 'Outs' seem to increase in frequency as each side gets near the children chosen last. ... Children have great difficulty spelling August. As children make mistakes those in seats say, 'No.' Teacher says, 'Man on third.' As child at board stops and thinks, teacher says, 'There's a time limit; you can't take too long, honey.' At last, after many children fail on August, a child gets it right, and returns grinning with pleasure to her seat. ... [Observer notes: Motivational level in this game seems terrific. They all seem to watch the board, know what's right or wrong, and seem quite keyed up. No lagging in moving from base to base.] .... Child who is now writing Thursday stops to think after first letter, and children snicker. Stops after another letter. More snickers. Gets word wrong. ... [Frequent signs of joy from the children when their side is right].

In the above, we may note the following as probable indeterminate responses: 1. anxiety and feelings of depreciation in the children chosen last by the captains; 2. feelings of self-depreciation and hostility in the students subject to snickers; and 3. anxieties aroused by the teacher's random phrases, 'get down on your knee', and 'keep your hands out of your pockets and anybody else's'. None of these responses could have been foreseen from a simple description of the game.

The next example is from a fifth-grade arithmetic lesson (Henry, 1957a, p. 123):

Boris had trouble reducing $\frac{12}{16}$ to lowest terms, and could get only as far as $\frac{6}{8}$. There was much excitement among the students who were watching him at the board. The teacher asked him quietly if that was as far as he could reduce it. She suggested he 'think'. There was much heaving up and down from the other children, all frantic to correct him. Boris looked pretty unhappy. The teacher was patient, quiet, ignoring the other students while concentrating with look and voice on Boris. ... At last, when Boris is unable to solve the problem the teacher turns to the class and says, 'Well, who can tell Boris what the number is?' There is forest of hands and the teacher calls on Peggy who says that 4 should be divided into both the numerator and denominator.

It is obvious that Boris's failure made it possible for Peggy to succeed, and, since the excited handwaving of the children indicates that they wanted to exploit Boris's predicament to succeed where he was failing, it appears that at least some of these children were learning to hope (covertly) for the failure of fellow-students. Having been reinforced in this way during long years of schooling, 'the 'I-hope-he-fails' attitude is common enough in the American character. It is an indeterminate, covert learning. If some teachers knew their students were learning to hope for the failure of fellow-students they would be horrified – provided they believed it was happening, since they certainly had no intention of teaching children to feel this way.

Many children have Boris's experience frequently during their school years, and possibly acquire a variety of indeterminate learnings over the long run. For example, they might learn hostility toward all successful children, fear of facing an audience, and hostility toward teachers, especially females (since most elementary-school teachers are females).

In addition to complementary, antithetical, and indeterminate responses there is still another *meta*-response, which I have called *pseudo*-complementary (Henry, 1955b). This is the response in which children, *without conviction*, give the teacher what they perceive she wants, and by so doing appear to be learning something they are not. In these circumstances, the lessons that are really learned are how to be docile – to give the teacher what she wants – and the importance of docility. This is not the same phenomenon as head-nodding in college, in rhythm to a professor's lecture, while inwardly denying the truth of everything he says. The latter is a feeble voice inwardly affirming autonomy, while *pseudo*-complementarity is real abandonment of it.

In sum, what a child learns (i.e. what responses are reinforced) is a result of the teacher's actions and intentions and of the child's own tendencies to respond. Out of the interplay between these grow complimentary, *pseudo*-complementary, antithetical and indeterminate responses on the part of the child. At any given time, any of the last three may be unintended by the teacher, and the only way for an observer to take account of them is by making an inventory of the response universe. Even then, the observer is still somewhat in the position of a man surveying space with a very small telescope: he can see some things and make shrewd guesses about others, but he also misses a great deal. However, in the absence of observation or inventory of the classroom response universe, we might imagine that all responses were complimentary – that nothing happens in a classroom except the children's answers to the teacher's questions. A theory of social and unintended learning must include antithetical, indeterminate and *pseudo*-complementary responses, and must anticipate them methodologically by an inventory of the response universe.

XI. WHAT SELF-CONCEPTIONS SEEM REINFORCED?

A teacher cannot avoid contributing to a student's self-conception, for human beings are self-concept-forming animals whose self-conceptions are in process of formation at every stage of learning. Among factors contributing to the formation of the self-conception are:

II.   How is the information communicated (teaching methods)?
- 27   *Through ego-inflation*
- 27(a) Through ego-deflation

IV.   How does the person being educated participate? (What is his attitude?)
- 11(b) Ridiculing peers
- 26(a) Hostile to peers
- 34. *By carping criticism*
- 35. *By praising work of peers*

V.   How does the educator participate? (What is his attitude?)
- 13. *Discouraging*
- 14. *Encouraging*
- 15. *Hostile, ridiculing, sarcastic, belittling*
- 18. *Personalizing*
- 19. *Depersonalizing*
- 23. *Accepting of child's spontaneous expressions*
- 24. *Rejecting of child's spontaneous expressions*
- 27. *Acts and/or talks as if child's self-image is fragile*
- 28. *Acts and/or talks as if child's self-image is irrelevant*
- 34. *Praises and rewards realistically*
- 36. *Critical (does not point out good things in student's work)*

IX.   What forms of discipline are used?

Of course, much of the conception of the self is formed during an early period of nurture within the family, but that early period is beyond the scope of this paper. Thus this section is confined to the question, 'What are the results, for the conception of the self, of the behaviour listed in sections II, IV, V, and IX?'

For anthropology, the importance of self-conceptions resides in the fact that they tend to be fairly uniform throughout each culture, and that social intercourse pivots on them. Thus the potlatch relationship between Kwakiutl chiefs is based on their recognition of each other's expansive self-conception (Benedict, 1946); and supreme conformity to peer-group norms among

American teenagers stems from their sense of personal inadequacy (Remmers and Radler, 1957, especially tables on pp. 80–
85). Our conclusion, similar to one derived in the preceding
section, is that in all cultures there must be an institutionalized
self-conception complementary to the cultural goals. This conclusion seems obvious enough, for it would certainly be disruptive if, in a culture like Hopi, where social life depends on severe
subordination of individual drive to group goals, people learned
a grandiose, individualized self-conception. A striking example of
the relation between a poor self-conception and cultural goals is
given by Mead (1939, part 2) for Manus. After describing the
free, generous, unfettered and independent life of the male children, she point out that this must be abandoned, and the adoles-
cent boy's spirit broken, at marriage, in order that he may take a
position at the bottom of adult society and start to learn the
workings of the economic system. Gradually, then, he will work
his way up to economic strength. Mead says (1939, part 2, pp.
208–9):

On all sides he must go humbly. He is poor, he has no home; *he is an
ignoramus.* . . . He enters an era of social eclipse. He cannot raise his
voice in a quarrel, he who as a small boy has told the old men in the
village to hold their noise. Then he was a gay and privileged child,
now he is the least and most despised of adults.
    All about him he sees two types of older men, those who have
mastered the economic system, become independent of their financial
backers, gone into the gift exchange for themselves, and those who
have slumped and who are still dependent nonentities, tyrannized
over by their younger brothers, forced to fish nightly to keep their
families in food. Those who have succeeded have done so by hard
dealing, close-fisted methods, stinginess, saving, ruthlessness. If he
would be like them, he must give up the good-natured ways of his
boyhood. . . . So the independence of his youth goes down before
the shame of poverty. [Thus the young married men are] meek,
abashed, sulky, skulking about the back doors of their rich relations'
houses. [Italics supplied.]

Thus, in Mead's analysis, the debased self-conception provides
the compensating dynamic of striving, so necessary for learning
and succeeding in the Manus socio-economic system.
    On the other hand, the physical rigours and trials (see II : 16 :

(a); 4 : 3(b) imposed on boys by many of the North American Indian tribes served to create a self-conception in which self-assurance and independence were conspicuous elements. Such self-conceptions were complimentary to the daring and independence of action demanded by a rigorous life.

XII. How does the process of formal instruction last?

It is very clear that one has to learn much more in American culture than in, say, Kaingáng culture (Henry, 1941). Therefore, the time spent being educated must be greater in cultures with elaborate technologies and ideologies than in those with simple ones. Indeed, the period of education might have had to be prolonged indefinitely in highly elaborated cultures, where there is so much to learn. However, this problem has been solved in all the great civilizations by apportionment of different activities to different social groups. Correlatively, status rank has been assigned to the latter in terms of the former. Coinciding with this, there has been, of necessity, a proportionate relationship between social status and the time spent in getting educated; persons of higher status tend to spend more time being educated than persons of lower status, and persons who are mobile upward spend more time in educating themselves than those who are not mobile upward.

Interestingly enough, these generalizations seem to hold even at relatively primitive levels of culture where there is little differentiation into structural classes or castes. A boy in any primitive society has to learn adult male subsistence techniques, and he often has to learn ceremonial too. If he wants to become a shaman or priest, he has to learn the techniques and ideologies of that occupation. The point of stating such truisms here is that *time* is expended to achieve a *change of status*, which is is regularly, but not always, a *rise* in status. In other words, commonly, though not universally, the higher one wishes to be in social status, the more time one has to spend educating oneself. We have already referred above to Pettit's analysis of the relation between education and the exercise of supernatural functions in primitive North America (1946, pp. 108 *et seq.*). Here it is only necessary to underscore that his material shows 1. the frequent correspondence between status change, for example advancing in the priesthood or in a secret society, and the length of time spent in being educated, and 2. the direct proportion between time spent in learning about the supernatural and the *elaboration* of priestly and related functions.

It seems likely that in all educational systems, literate as well as non-literate, some assumptions must be made about *pace*. In Samoa nobody must learn too fast (Mead, 1939, part 1, pp. 33, 35), while in Taleland rapid learning is admired (Fortes, 1938, p. 13). The pace at which education is conducted is, of course, related to the cultural dictate about how much of a life-span should be given to education. But a great deal of further research is necessary in cultures other than our own on the matter of pace and its relation to total cultural configurations.

Summary and conclusions: some ancient and abiding characteristics of human education

1. Use of reward stimuli to learning: primarily praise, appreciation, and status elevation.

2. Use of pain stimuli to learning: ridicule, accusation, physical pain, physical confinement (restriction of movement).

3. Use of role-occupant as role-instructor (teaching of archery by archers, of agriculture by farmers, of warfare by warriors, of mathematics by practitioners of mathematics, of carpentry by carpenters, etc.) This has undergone radical change since the emergence of modern mass education.

4. In high civilizations: low status of teachers, unless they teach sacred matters.

5. In high civilizations: a correlation between (*a*) love of knowledge for its own sake, with (*b*) status of teachers, and with (*c*) the interest of students in learning.

6. Confinement of creativity to gifted individuals (creativity never a mass phenomenon).

7. Absence of the assumption of a natural impulse to learn. (This does not mean that children are not everywhere naturally investigative, but there is no evidence that children will not lose interest in learning when it requires work.)

8. Congruence of status change with education, coupled with definite marks of adult recognition of status change.

9. Unity of the social sphere, including education, in non-literate cultures outside the stream of industrialization.

The main point deriving from this cross-cultural study of education is that *homo sapiens* learned long ago that there is no such thing as 'natural maturation' in a social sense, and that the central problem for human beings is the adaptation of each new generation to culture. This includes learning the techniques for survival each particular culture has found reliable.

It would appear that, on the whole, adult *homo sapiens* has rarely taken it for granted that children could or would just naturally learn by spontaneous imitation. At the same time, the children of *homo sapiens* have not assumed that they would just naturally grow into adulthood. Rather, children have always been aware that they have to validate their status as adults by learning adult techniques from older teachers. It follows that *homo sapiens* has been born on a kind of status machine – a status escalator or a status treadmill, depending on the culture – from which there has rarely been any socially acceptable escape. Thus, throughout his historic course, *homo sapiens* has been a 'status seeker', and the pathway he has had to follow, by compulsion, has been education. Furthermore, he has always had to rely on those superior to him in knowledge and social status to enable him to raise his own status. On the other hand, it is not clear that adults have always assumed that children would naturally wish to be adult. Over and over again, the data shows that children have had to be urged up the status ladder by rewards, punishments, and other even more complex devices. From the point of view of the adults this is absolutely necessary, for otherwise the children would remain dependent and disgracefully deviant in other ways. From the standpoint of the child, he must climb the status ladder or suffer the consequences of dependence and deviance. It is likely, meanwhile, that this compulsion and the inner conflict involved leave a lasting impression on the child, so that as a mature adult these memories can provide a fertile soil for social change, for if conditions arise that seem to provide an opportunity to eliminate the sources of the pains of childhood growth, adults may be happy to take advantage of the situation and push for change, often, perhaps, not knowing the real sources of their readiness.

Also deriving from this study is an insight into the enormous effort that *homo sapiens* has put into narrowing the perceptual sphere of the individual. To this end he has employed ridicule, praise, torture, admonition, etc., etc. with all the ingenuity his great brain has been able to devise. Thus, though *homo sapiens* has been also *homo inquisitor* – man the curious, the inquirer – he has always worried that his careful arrangement of cultural patterns would be destroyed if he *learned without limit*.

Finally, protecting himself from *inundation by stimuli*, *homo sapiens* has erected the categories of his languages and his culture patterns. Of course, in the long run these intellectual walls crumble because of the inherently variable mental constitution of *homo sapiens*, because many devices he uses for narrowing the perceptual sphere are unrewarding and self-defeating, because of the polyphasic nature of human learning, and because of the indeterminate factors that are always present in human learning. Thus, the dialectic of man's effort to understand the universe has always decreed that he should be alternately pulled forward by what has made him *homo inquisitor* and held back by the fear that if he knew too much he would destroy himself, i.e. his culture. So it is that though language has been an instrument with which man might cleave open the universe and peer within, it has also been an iron matrix that bound his brain to ancient modes of thought. And thus it is that though man has poured what he knows into his culture patterns, they have also frozen round him and held him fast.

References

American Journal of Sociology (1913), vol. 18, entire issue.

Ammar, H. (1954), *Growing up in an Egyptian Village*, Routledge & Kegan Paul.

Anderson, H. H., and Brewer, H. M. (1945), *Studies of Teachers' Classroom Personalities*, vol. 1, Stanford University Press.

Anderson, H. H., and Brewer, J. (1946), *Studies of Teachers' Classroom Personalities*, vol. 2, Stanford University Press.

Anderson, H. H., Brewer, J., and Reed, M. F. (1946), *Studies of Teachers' Classroom Personalities*, vol. 3, Stanford University Press.

Aristotle (1925), *The Works of Aristotle Translated into English*, vol. 9, Clarendon Press.

Bayne-Powell, R. (1939), *The English Child in the Eighteenth Century*, E. P. Dutton.

Belo, J. (1949, *Bali: Rangda and Barong*, J. J. Augustin.

Belo, J. (1954), 'Balinese children's drawings', in M. Mead and M. Wolfenstein (eds.), *Childhood in Contemporary Cultures*, pp. 52–69, University of Chicago Press.

Benedict, R. (1938), 'Continuities and discontinuities in cultural conditioning', *Psychiatry*, vol. 1, pp. 161–7.

Benedict, R. (1946), *Patterns of Culture*, Penguin.

Bertalanffy, L. von (1950), 'The theory of open systems in physics and biology', *Science*, vol. 111, p. 23.

Beuford, W. H. (1935), *Germany in the Eighteenth Century*, Cambridge University Press.

Calhoun, A. W. (1945), *A Social History of the American Family*, Barnes & Noble.

Chaudhuri, N. C. (1951), *The Autobiography of an Unknown Indian*, Macmillan.

Chiang, Y. (1952), *A Chinese Childhood*, John Day.

Childs, H. L. (1938), *The Nazi Primer*, Harper & Row.

Counts, G. and Lodge, N. P. (1947), *I Want to be Like Stalin*, John Day.

Dennis, W. (1940), *The Hopi Child*, Appleton-Century-Crofts.

Durkheim, E. (1947), *Elementary Forms of the Religious Life*, Free Press.

Eggan, D. (1956), 'Instruction and affect in Hopi cultural continuity', *Southwestern J. Anthrop.*, vol. 12, pp. 338–65.

Du Bois, C. (1944), *The People of Alor*, University of Minnesota Press.

Elwin, V. (1939), *The Baiga*, Murray.

Firth, R. (1936), *We, the Tikopia*, American Book Co.

Fortes, M. (1938), *Social and Psychological Aspects of Education in Taleland*, Oxford University Press.

Freud, S. (1955), *A General Introduction to Psychoanalysis*, Perma Books.

Fuchs, S. (1950), *The Children of Hari*, Verlag Herold.

Gorer, G. (1938), *Himalayan Village*, Michael Joseph.

Gray, W. S., Monroe, M., Artley, A. S., and Arbuthnot, M. H. (1956), *More Streets and Roads*, Scott, Foresman.

Hart, C. W. M. (1955), 'Contrasts between prepubertal and postpubertal education', in G. Spindler (ed.), *Education and Anthropology*, pp. 127–45, Stanford University Press.

Henry, J. (1941), *Jungle People*, J. J. Augustin.

Henry, J., and Boggs, J. W. (1952), 'Child rearing, culture and the natural world', *Psychiatry*, vol. 15, pp. 261–71.

Henry, J. (1955a), 'Culture, education and communications theory', in G. Spindler (ed.), *Education and Anthropology*, pp. 188–207, Stanford University Press.

Henry, J. (1955b), 'Docility, or giving teacher what she wants', *J. soc. Iss*, vol. 11, pp. 33–41.

Henry, J. (1957a), 'Attitude organization in elementary school classrooms', *Amer. J. Orthopsychiatry*, vol. 27, pp. 117–33.

Henry, J. (1957b), Working paper on creativity, *Harvard Educ. Rev.*, vol. 27, pp. 148–55.

Henry, J. (1958), 'The personal community and its invariant properties', *Amer. Anthrop.*, vol. 60, pp. 827–31.

Henry, J. (1959), 'The problem of spontaneity, initiative and creativity in suburban classrooms', *Amer. J. Orthopsychiatry*, vol. 29, pp. 266–79.

Hollingshead, A. B. (1949), *Elmtown's Youth*, Wiley.

Holmberg, A. R. (1950), *Nomads of the Long Bow*, Smithsonian Institution, Institute of Social Anthropology, publication no. 10, Government Printing Office.

Hutton, J. H. (1946, *Caste in India*, Cambridge University Press.

Ilin, M. (1931), *New Russia's Primer*, Houghton Mifflin.

Kahl, J. (1957), *The American Class Structure*, Holt, Rinehart & Winston.

Kluckhohn, F. (1951), 'Dominant and variant cultural value orientations', *Soc. Wel. Forum*, pp. 97–113.

Leighton, D., and Kluckhohn, C. (1948), *Children of the People*, Harvard University Press.

Leonard, O., and Loomis, G. P. (1941), *Culture of a Contemporary Rural Community: El Servito, New Mexico*, Department of Agriculture, Bureau of Agricultural Economics Rural Life Studies no. 1, Government Printing Office.

Macgregor, G. (1946), *Warriors Without Weapons*, University of Chicago Press.

Malinowski, B. (1943), 'The pan-African problem of culture contact', *Amer. J. Sociol.*, vol. 48, pp. 619–65.

Matthan, T. (1905), *The Act of Touch*, Longman.

Mead, M. (1928), *Coming of Age in Samoa*, Mentor Books; Penguin, 1943.

Mead, M. (1939), *From The South Seas*, William Morrow.

Mead, M. (1943), 'Our educational emphasis in primitive perspective', *Amer. J. Sociol.*, vol. 48, pp. 633–9.

Mead, M., and Bateson, G. (1942), *Balinese Character*, Academy of Sciences.

Mead, M., and Bateson, G. (1942), *Balinese Character*, Academy *Cultures*, University of Chicago Press.

Miller, N., and Dollard, J. (1941), *Social Learning and Imitation*, Yale University Press.

Pavlov, I. P. (1928), *Lectures on Conditional Reflexes*, International Publishers.

Pettitt, G. A. (1946), *Primitive Education in North America*, University of California Press.

Pirenne, H. (1937), *Economic and Social History of Medieval Europe*, Harcourt, Brace & World.

Rabin, B. (1959), 'Teacher use and directive language', *Educational Leadership*, vol. 17, pp. 31–4.

Radcliffe-Brown, A. R. (1948), *The Andaman Islanders*, Free Press.

Raum, O. F. (1940), *Chagga Childhood*, Oxford University Press.

Remmers, H. H., and Radler, D. H. (1957), *The American Teenager*, Bobbs-Merrill.

Savery, C. (1942), *Luck and Pluck*, D. C. Heath.

Simmons, J. W. (1942), *Sun Chief: The Autobiography of a Hopi Indian*, Yale University Press.

Simpson, G. G. (1951), *The Meaning of Evolution*, Mentor Books.

Social Welfare Forum (1951), *Social Welfare Forum*, Columbia University Press.

Spindler, G. (ed.) (1955), *Education and Anthropology*, Stanford University Press.

Spindler, G. (1959), *The Transmission of American Culture*, Harvard University Press.

Spiro, M. (1958), *Children of the Kibbutz*, Harvard University Press.

Sunley, R. (1954), 'Early nineteenth-century American literature on child rearing', in M. Mead and M. Wolfenstein (eds.), *Childhood in Contemporary Cultures*, pp. 150–67, University of Chicago Press.

Thompson, E. T. (1943), 'Comparative education in colonial areas with special reference to plantation and mission frontiers', *Amer. J. Sociol.*, vol. 48, pp. 710–21.

Tinbergen, N. (1951), *The Study of Instinct*, Clarendon Press.

Toynbee, A. J. (1953), *Greek Civilization and Character*, Mentor Books.

Warner, W. L. (1937), *A Black Civilization*, Harper & Row.

Warner, W. L., Havighurst, R. J., and Loeb, M. R. (1944), *Who Shall Be Educated?*, Harper & Row.

Watkins, M. H. (1943), 'The West African "bush" school', *Amer. J. Sociol.*, vol. 48, pp. 666–75.

Whiting, J. (1941), *Becoming a Kwoma*, Yale University Press.

Williams, S. W. (1849), *The Middle Kingdom*, vol. 1, Wiley, 3rd edn.

Yang, M. C. (1945), *A Chinese Village*, Columbia University Press.

Zborowski, M., and Herzog, E. (1952), *Life is with People*, International Universities Press.

JULES HENRY was born in New York City in 1904. He died in St. Louis, Missouri, on September 23, 1969. He studied under Franz Boas and Ruth Benedict at Columbia University, where he received his doctorate in anthropology in 1936. Dr. Henry taught at Columbia University, the University of Chicago, and until his death at Washington University in St. Louis.

He was a Research Associate at the Sonia Shankman Orthogenic School and was a Fellow at the Center for Advanced Study in the Behavioral Sciences at Stanford. He also served as consultant to the National Institute of Mental Health and the World Health Organization, among others, as well as a number of psychiatric hospitals. His articles have been widely published in professional and general journals. He is the author of "Doll Play of Pilagá Indian Children" (a monograph), *Jungle People, Culture Against Man*, and *Pathways to Madness*.

Dr. Henry married Zunia Lotte Gechtman; their daughter, Phyllis, is married to Peter Kingsmill.

DUE